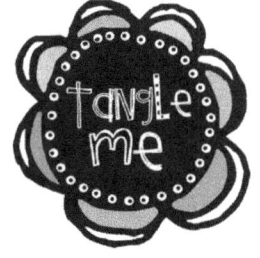

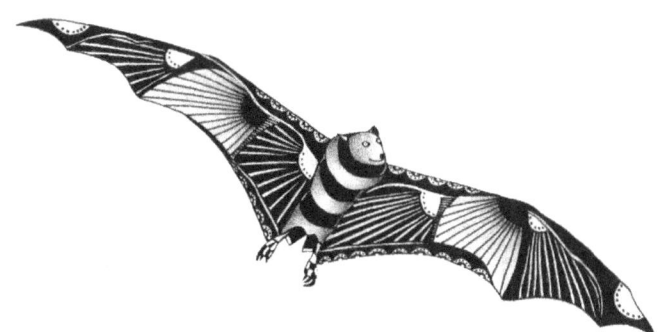

I hope you enjoy tangling these animals as much as I did when creating them for you and your children.

Lesley

www.engagedinart.com

DISCLAIMER

Tangle Me - Aussie Animals © 2015 Lesley Smitheringale

INTRODUCTION

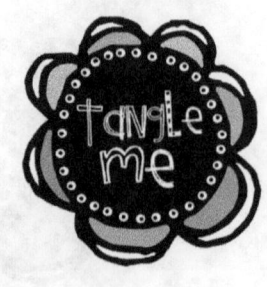

This book has been designed for everyone who loves to draw and tangle.

The Zentangle® Method is an easy-to-learn, relaxing, and fun way to create beautiful images by drawing structured patterns. It was created by Rick Roberts and Maria Thomas. "Zentangle" is a registered trademark of Zentangle, Inc. True Zentangles are not supposed to represent anything. They are abstract, unplanned, black and white patterned drawings which can be viewed from any angle with no right or wrong way of drawing or looking at them.

The activities in this book are not the true traditional zentangles as described above but are zentangle-inspired artworks.

HOW TO USE THIS BOOK

People of all ages and artistic abilities can use this book as the basics are covered at the beginning for younger artists who are just learning how to make patterns and the finished resource examples are for more advanced artists and tanglers.

Teachers can use this book to teach students about line, shape, pattern, repetition, counterchange, linear tone, direction and bonus info is included about the 12 Aussie animals.

I hope you enjoy tangling the animals!

Lesley

www.engagedinart.com

About the Artist

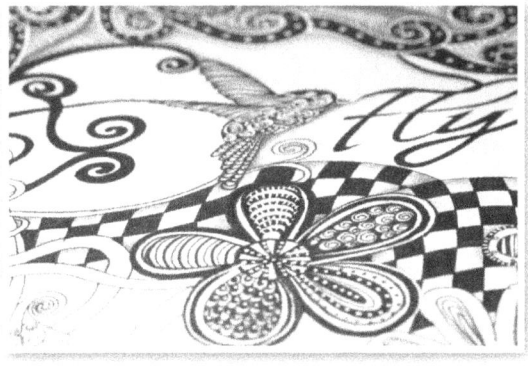

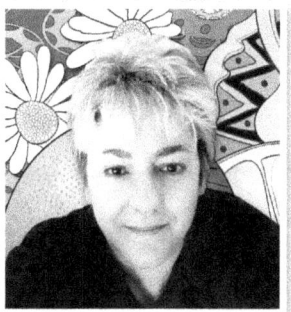

Lesley Smitheringale

Lesley lives and works in her home studio in the Redlands area of Queensland, Australia. She was born in Glasgow, Scotland where she obtained a BA with honours in Design at Glasgow School of Art. She then did further training to become an art teacher and after teaching for twenty years to Middle and High School students, Lesley took the plunge and decided to work for herself. She currently produces her own artwork where she embraces both traditional and digital media.

Lesley produces a range of hand-made, nature inspired giftware in her Oz Wildlife Studio Shop and also provides art and craft resources on her Engaged in Art Website where she acts as a "virtual" art teacher, sharing the techniques and creative ideas she has learned on her art journey.

Lesley also runs a private Group on Facebook called "Colouring and Tangling" where she provides a virtual meeting place for adults who love to colour and produce zentangle-inspired artworks.

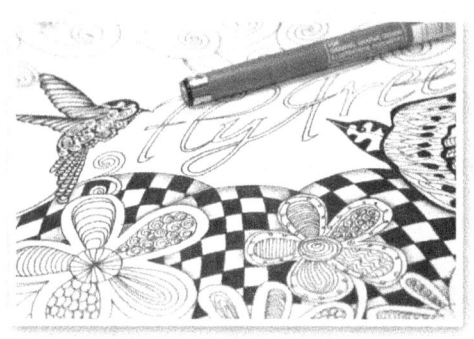

She also runs workshops for adults in her home studio "Tea & Tangling" and "Coffee & Colouring" for those who live in the Brisbane | Redlands area of Queensland.

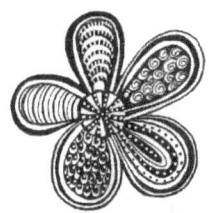

www.ozwildlifestudio.com
www.engagedinart.com
https://www.facebook.com/groups/colouringandtangling

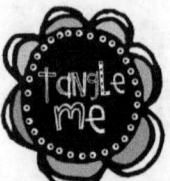

LINES

Let's start with a line. How many different ways can we draw a line?

———————————— straight line

～～～～～～～ wavy line

～～～～～ another wavy line - this looks like an ocean wave

ﾍﾍﾍﾍﾍﾍ zig zag line

eeeeeee a looped line - this looks like a twisted phone cord

ｗｗｗｗ higher wavy line

wwww scribbly line

ＶＶＶＶ high zig zag line - these look like joined triangles

let's change the direction of our lines

vertical lines   horizontal lines   dashed or broken lines

diagonal lines

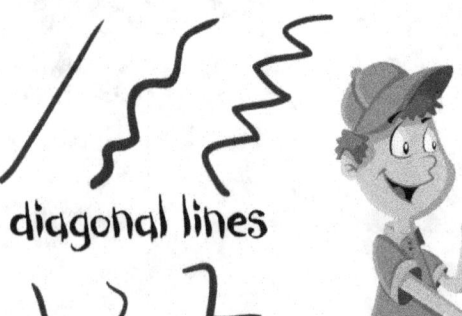

Task
On the next page draw as many different types of lines as you can think of. Make some of them straight, some curved, some broken and change the direction of the lines.

 LINES

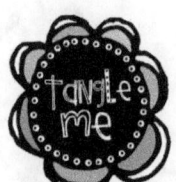 # CIRCLES, OVALS AND SPIRALS

Now let's draw circles, ovals and spirals.
How many different ways can we draw them?

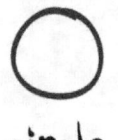 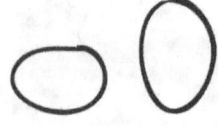 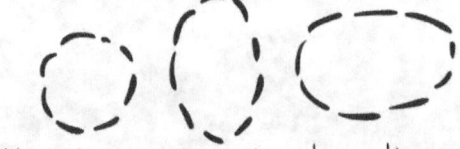 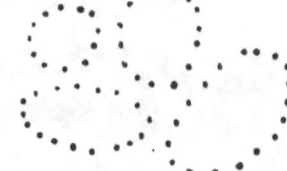

circle   ovals   with dashed or broken lines

dotted lines

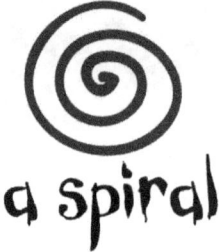

a spiral

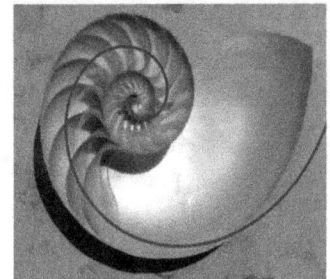

The nautilus shell has
a spiral pattern on it.

a spiral is a curved line which goes around and around
in a circular direction.

it can be tricky to draw a spiral
let's break it down into steps

C   start by drawing the letter c

         continue drawing a curve
         around the letter c

         continue the curve again

         stop your spiral after doing
         a few curves

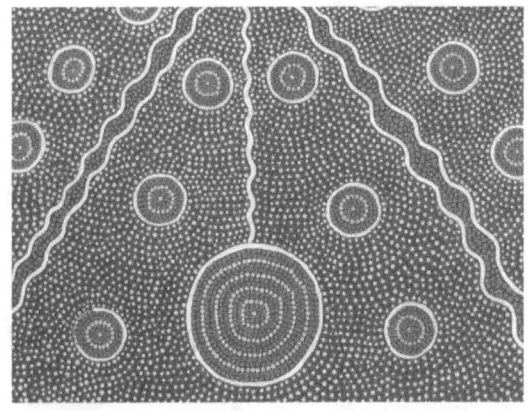

This is an example of Aboriginal art
where the artist has used wavy lines,
big circles and tiny circles (dots).

now try drawing a square spiral

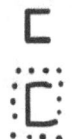 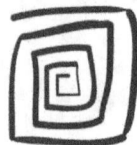

 this looks like a maze

Task

On the next page
practice drawing
circles and spirals.

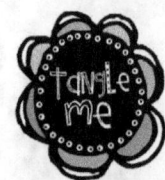

LINEAR PATTERNS

Now we are going to repeat the lines, circles, ovals and spirals to make patterns.

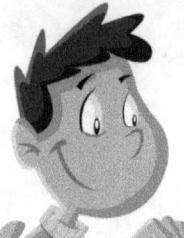

A pattern is a mark, line or shape which is repeated over and over again and because we are drawing lines, these are called LINEAR PATTERNS.

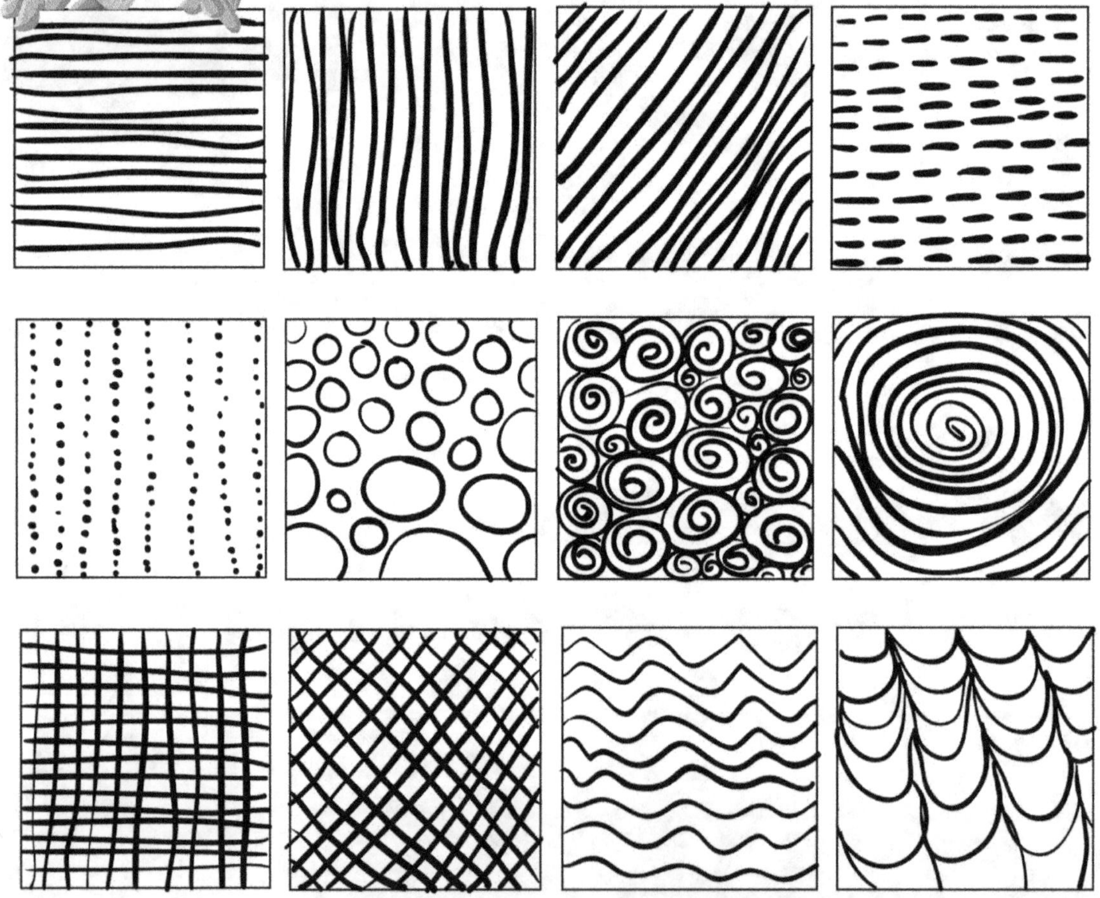

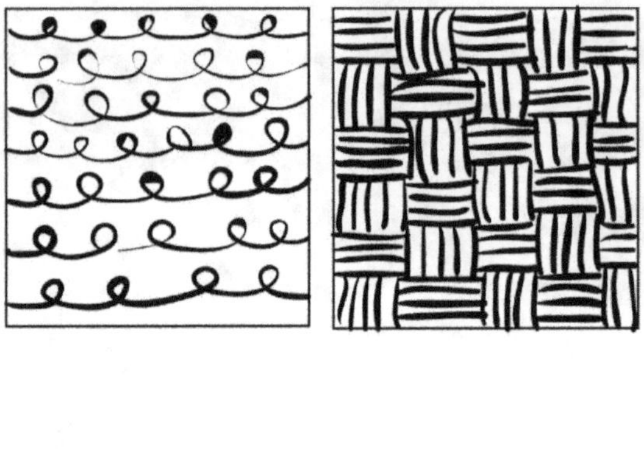

Task: On the next sheet, fill the boxes with lines, circles and spirals repeated in as many different ways you can. Try to come up with your own ideas rather than simply copying these examples.

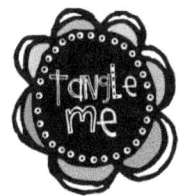

LINEAR PATTERNS

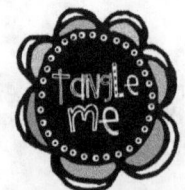

BLaCK aND WHITe

We are now going to create shapes from our linear patterns by filling in some solid black areas.

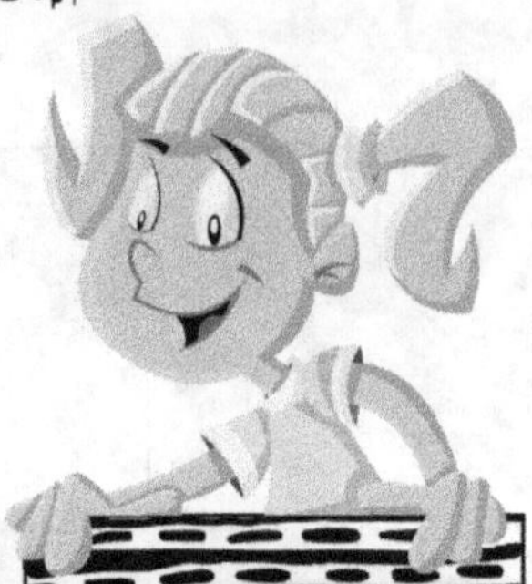

We want to have a good balance of black and white.

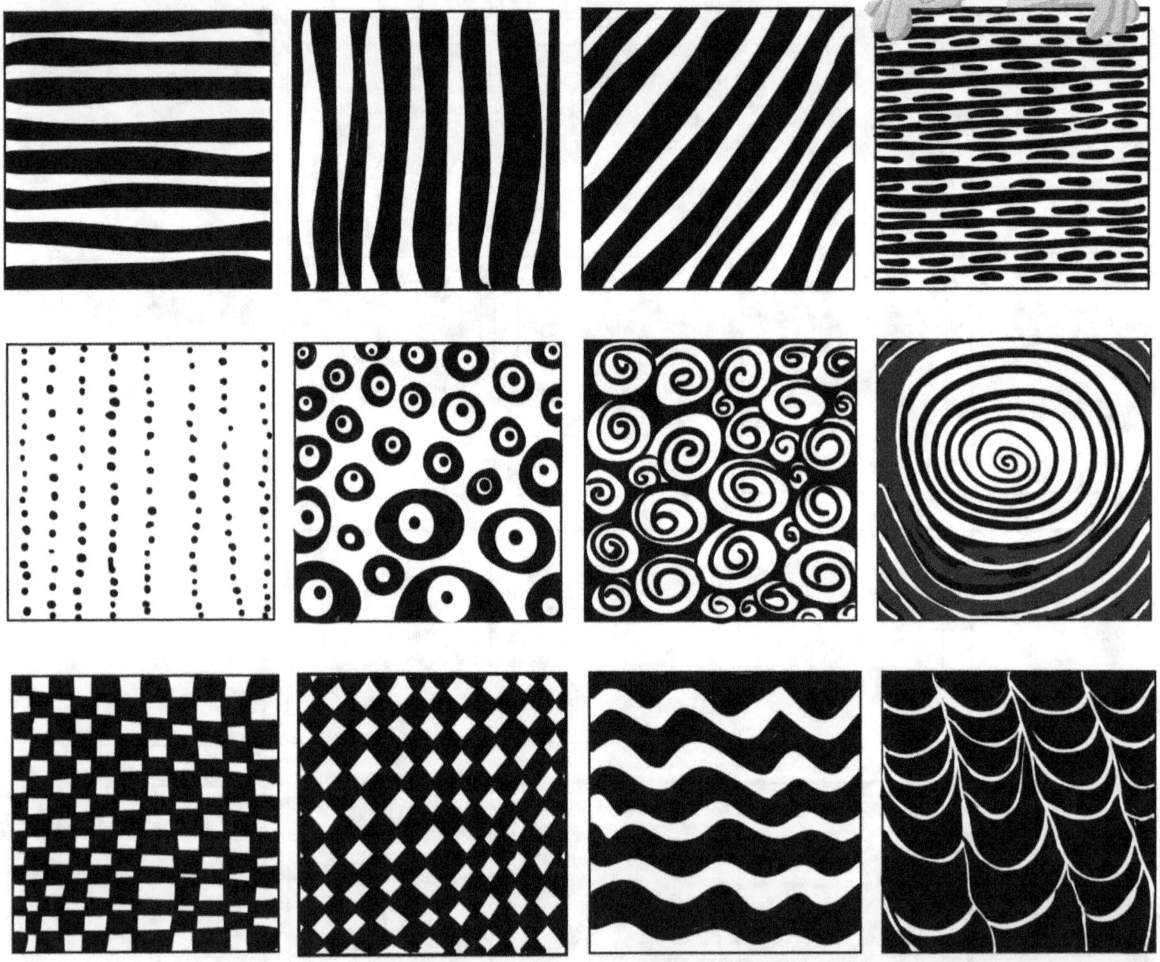

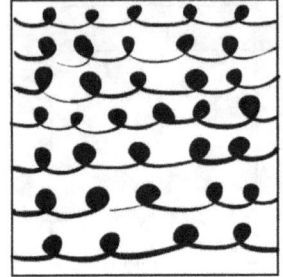

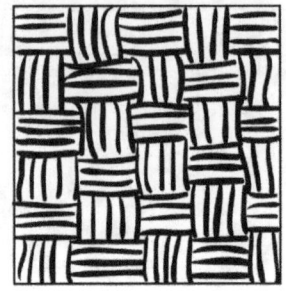

Task: Using the last sheet of linear patterns you created inside the squares, fill in some of the areas black using a sharpie pen to create a good balance of black and white areas.

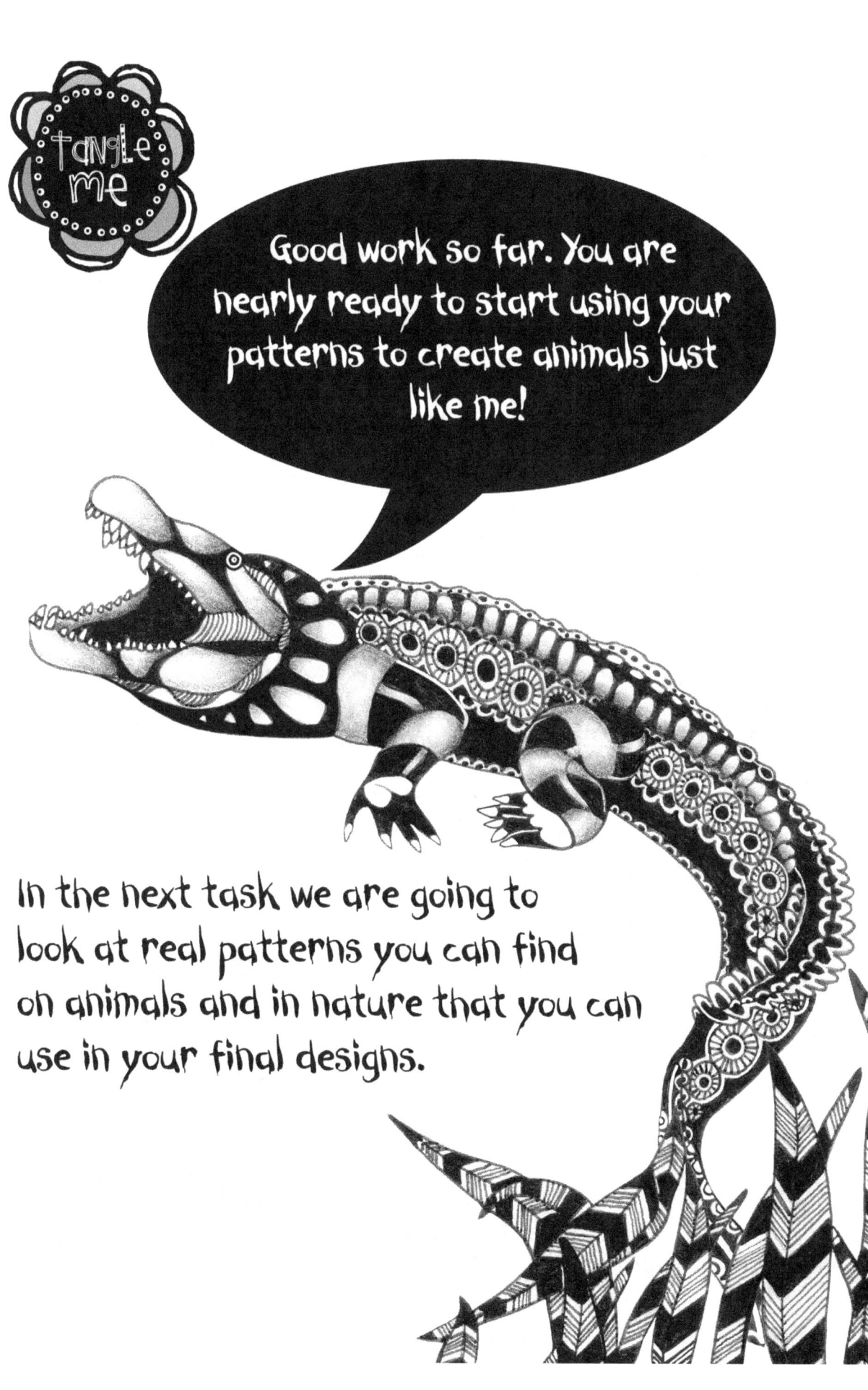

Good work so far. You are nearly ready to start using your patterns to create animals just like me!

In the next task we are going to look at real patterns you can find on animals and in nature that you can use in your final designs.

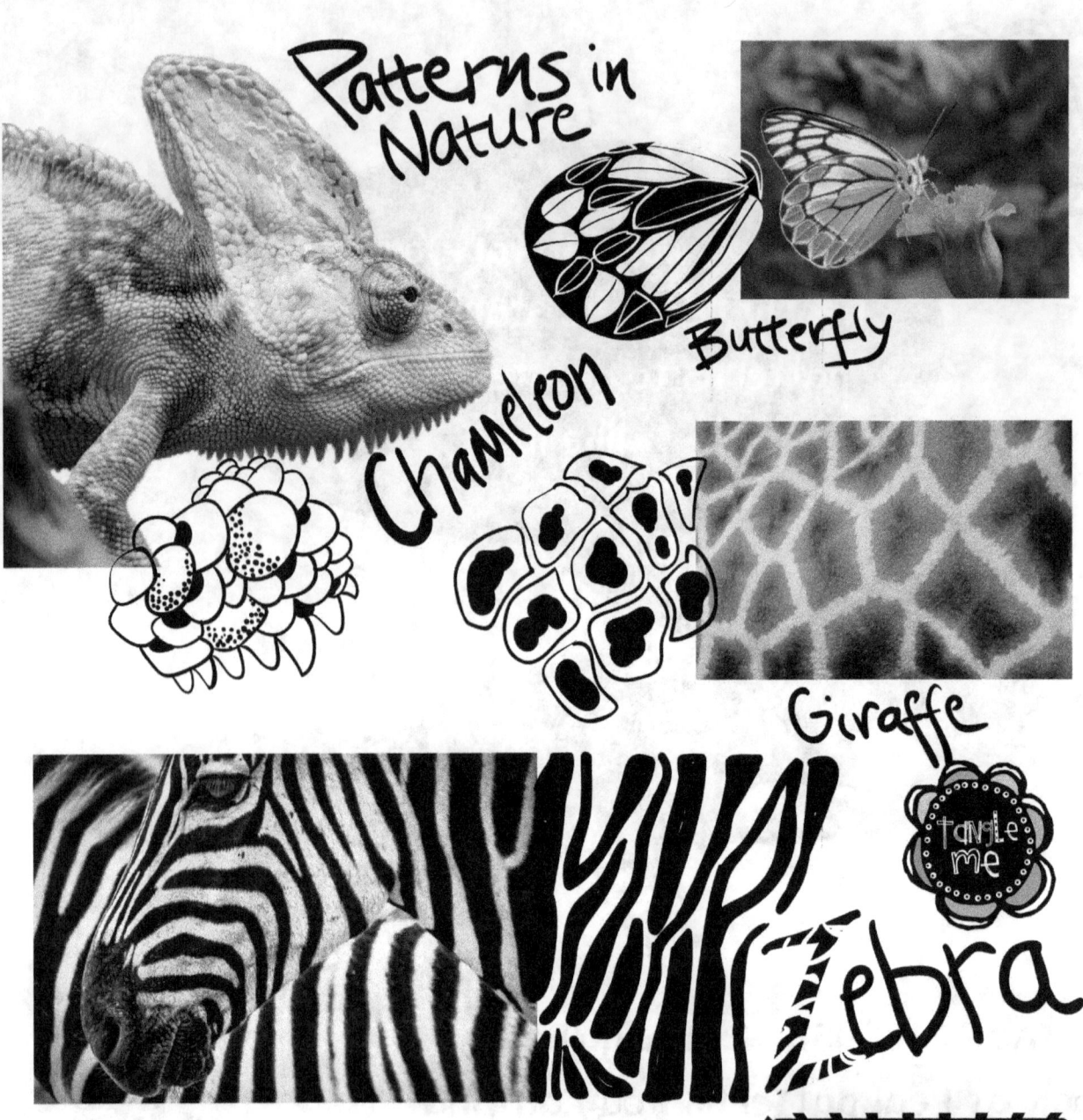

Patterns in Nature

Chameleon

Butterfly

Giraffe

tangle me

Zebra

Task

Find pictures of patterns in nature which could be on animals, birds, shells, insects, trees, leaves etc Cut and paste them on the next page and then draw the patters in black and white.

Snails

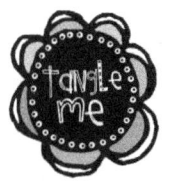

PATTERNS IN NATURE

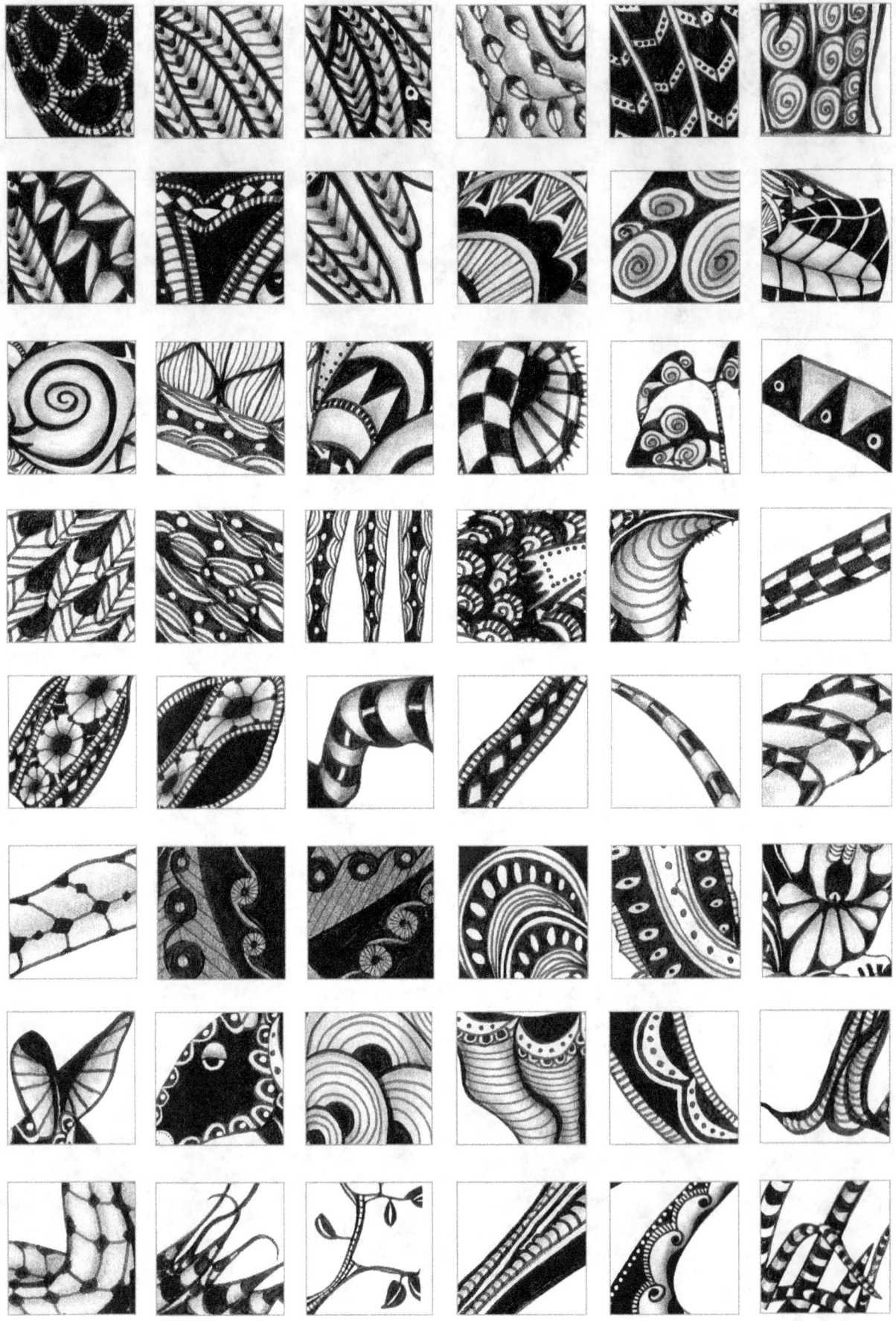

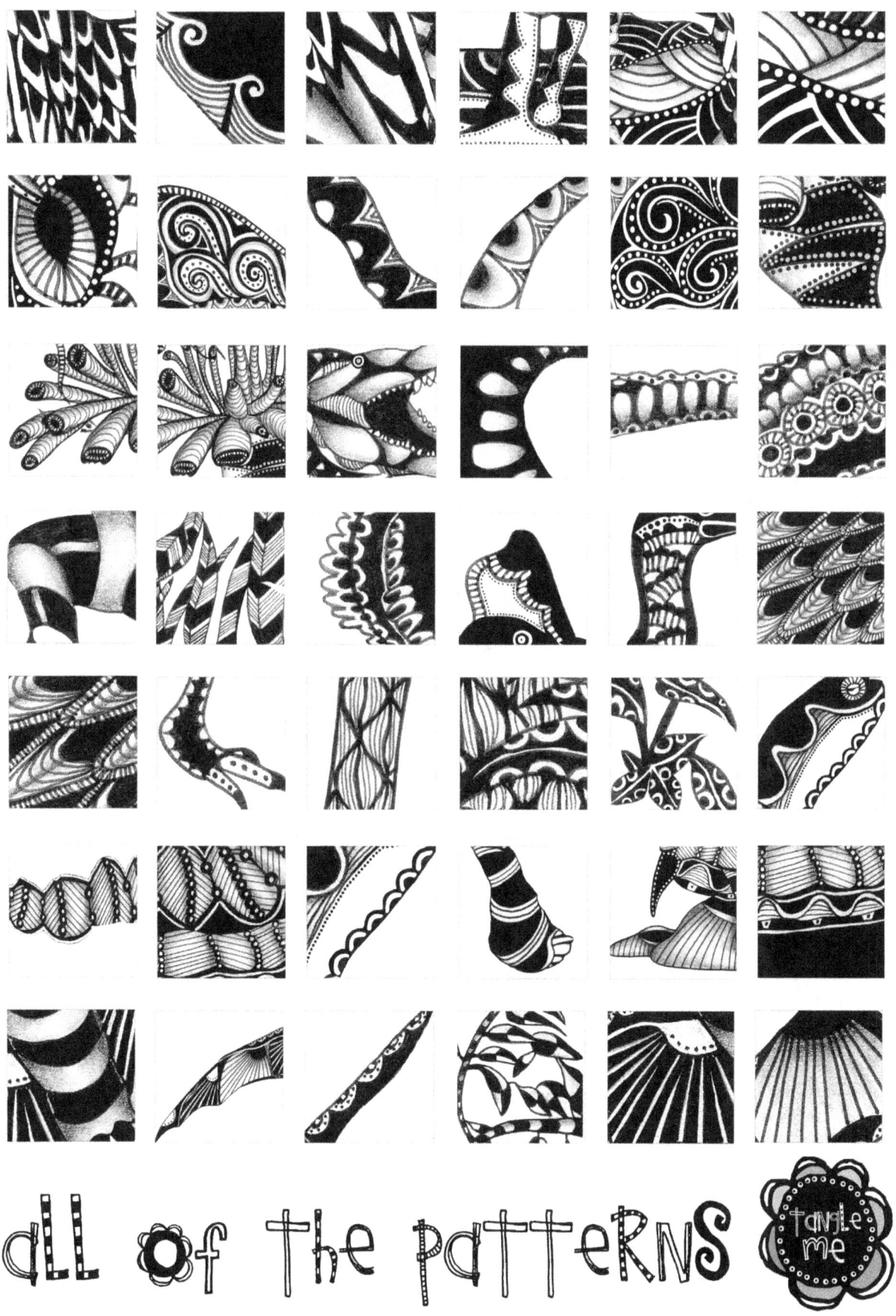

all of the patterns

MATERIALS REQUIRED

Congratulations! You are now ready to begin tangling 12 animals using the greyscale templates, your own patterns and the example patterns provided.

Recommended Materials

*A set of permanent black pens in a range of thicknesses - the best ones are the pigment ink pens which are water resistant (I have used Artline, Faber Castell Pitt Artist pens and Unipin pens purchased from officeworks)
*White Pigment Ink Pen [for correcting mistakes and touch ups]
[you can use Sharpies but I have read that the ink fades to brown after a while]
*HB and 2B pencil
*eraser
* Tortillion [paper stump/blender] for softening the pencil shading

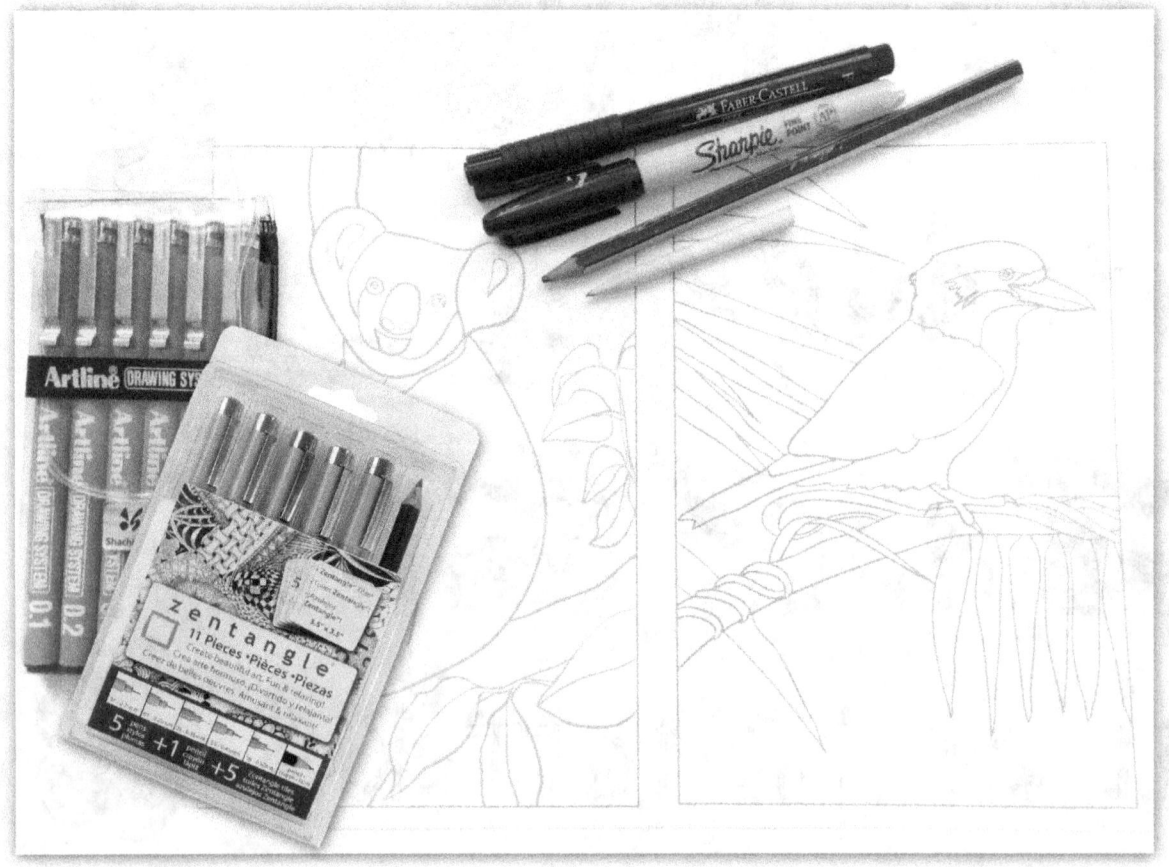

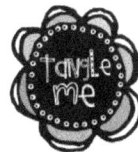

TIPS

Before you start, here are some important things to consider when tangling.

1. Subdivide the animal using a pencil into sections first which will contain different patterns. In the koala, the head, ears, arms & body have been subdivided and contain different patterns.

2. Try to make the placement and direction of your patterns follow the natural shapes of the animal. Notice in the tangled koala that the patterns on the koala's arm are curved to follow the natural shape. The same for the leaves pattern on the body etc.

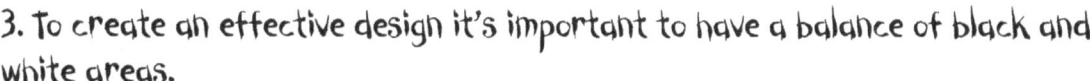

3. To create an effective design it's important to have a balance of black and white areas.

4. If you make a mistake, don't panic. Use the white gel pen or a white out correction pen to white out any mistakes. You can carefully go back over these areas with the black pens if necessary.

5. Use the white gel pen to create fine details such as dots or highlights on the animals' eyes.

6. To create a slight 3-dimensional effect on certain white areas, draw in a little bit of pencil then blend it out with the tortillion or paper blender. This is very easy to do and really makes your tangles pop! Have a look at the kookaburra.

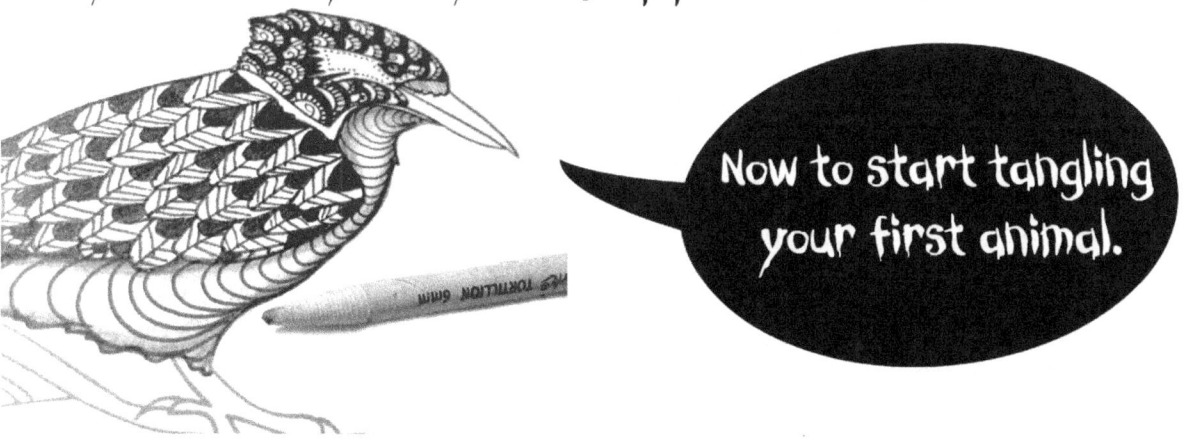

Now to start tangling your first animal.

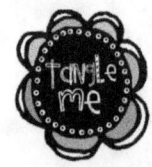 # tangle a Butterfly

For your first tangled creature which is going to be a butterfly, the steps have been included to help you get into the swing of things.

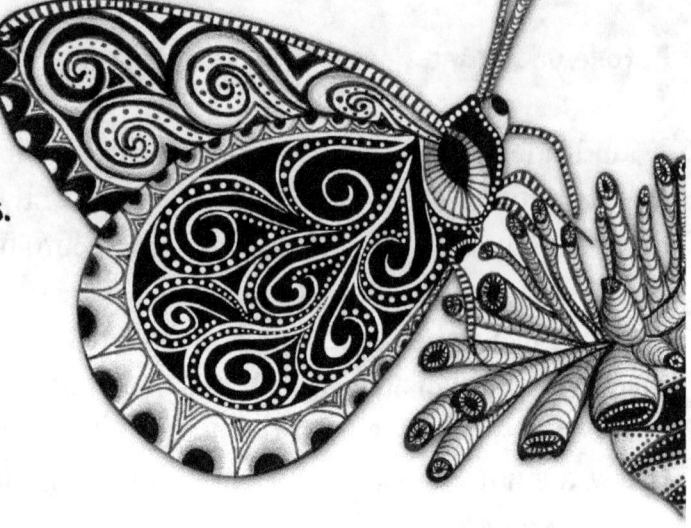

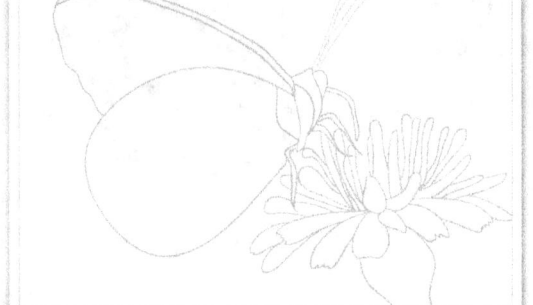

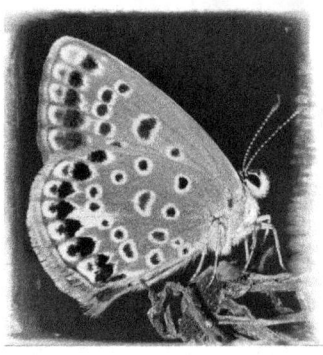

1. The original greyscale template

2. Using a pencil start to subdivide the butterfly and think about what patterns you are going to use.

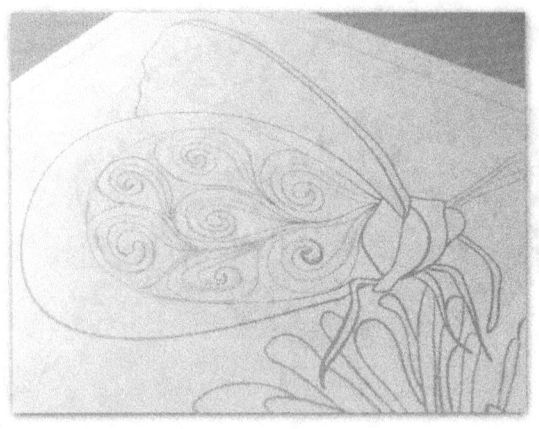

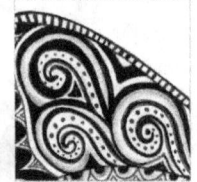

3. A spiral pattern has been pencilled in on one of the butterfly's wings.

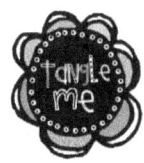

TANGLE A BUTTERFLY

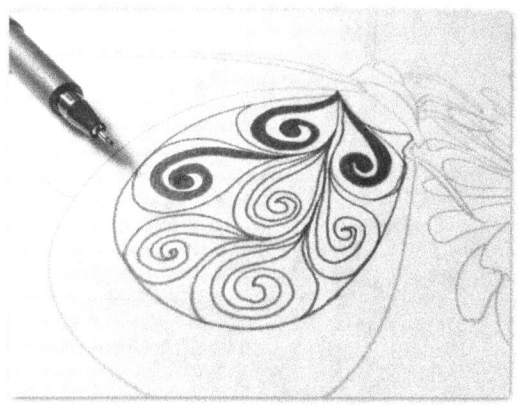

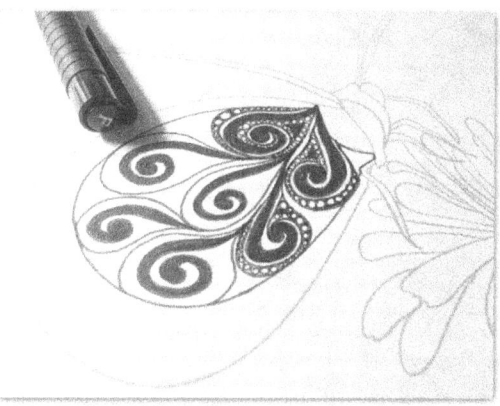

4. Starting to fill in the black areas of the spiral pattern with a pen.

TIP: for a more precise edge, draw the outline of the shape first with the pen before filling in the solid colour.

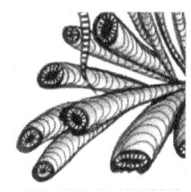 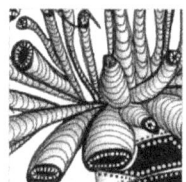 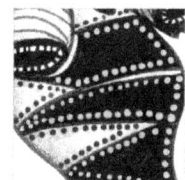

5. Adding detail to the pattern.

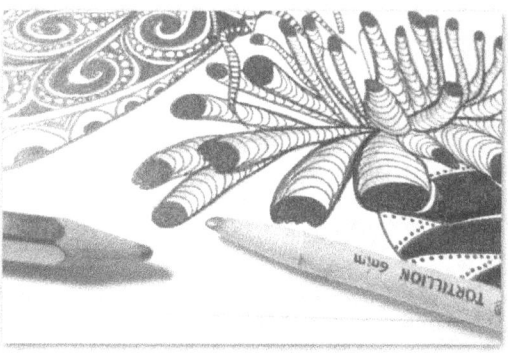

6. A tubular pattern on the flower stems and shading with pencil and blending with the tortillion to create a 3-dimensional effect.

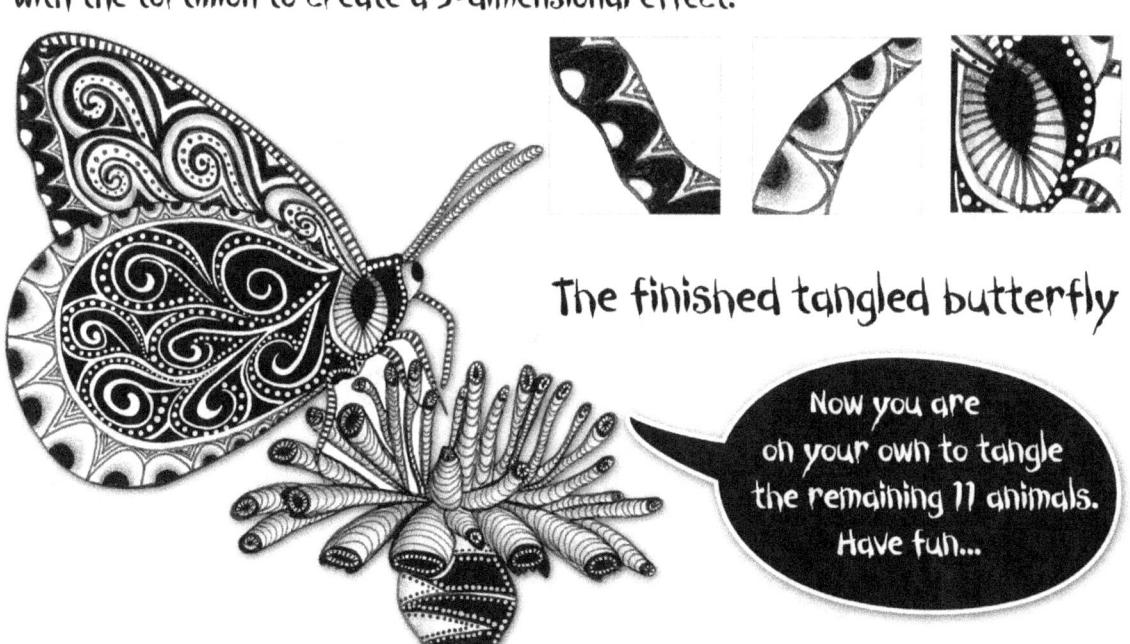

The finished tangled butterfly

Now you are on your own to tangle the remaining 11 animals. Have fun...

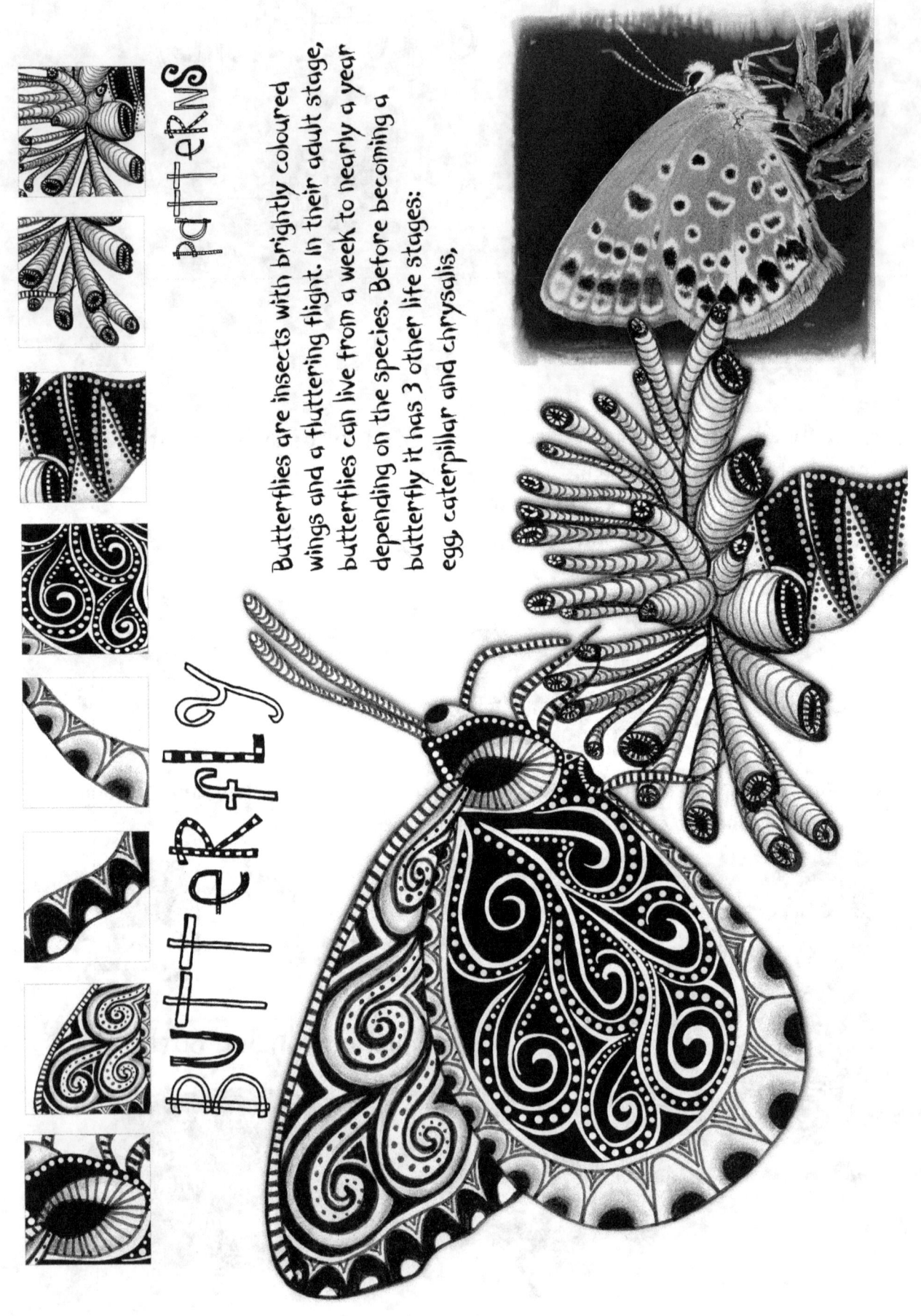

BUTTERFLY

PATTERNS

Butterflies are insects with brightly coloured wings and a fluttering flight. In their adult stage, butterflies can live from a week to nearly a year depending on the species. Before becoming a butterfly it has 3 other life stages: egg, caterpillar and chrysalis.

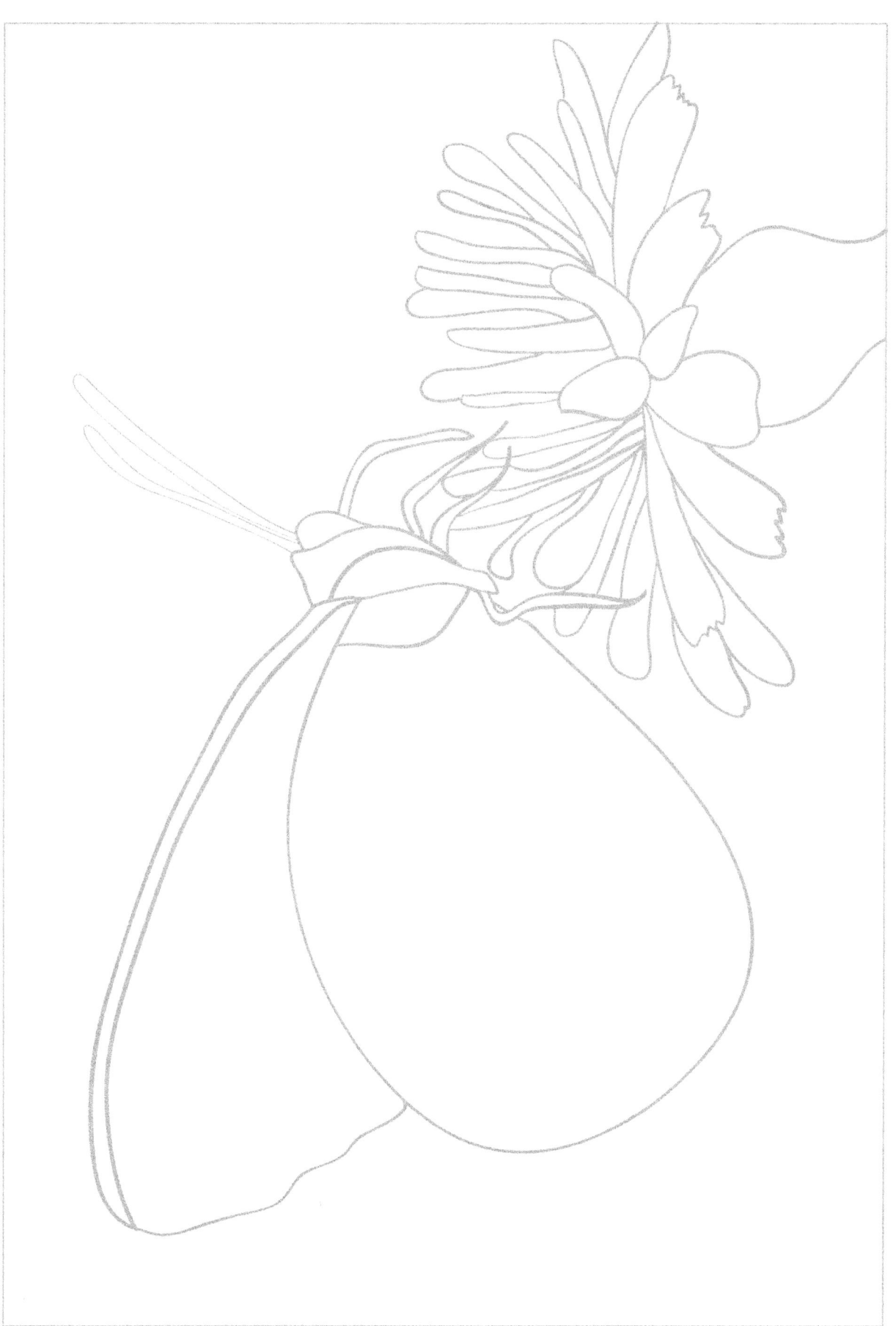

tangle a koala

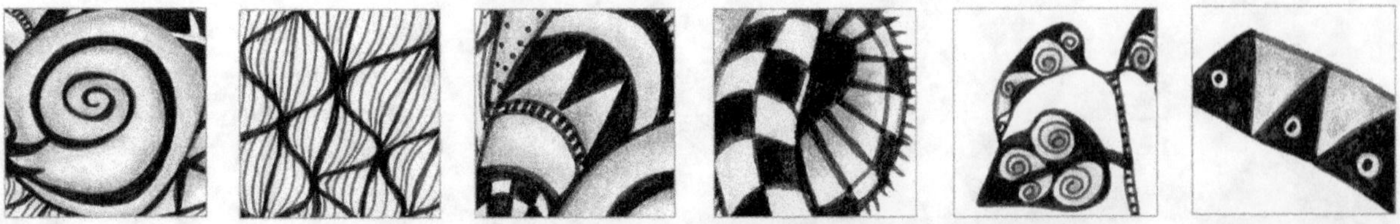

PATTERNS

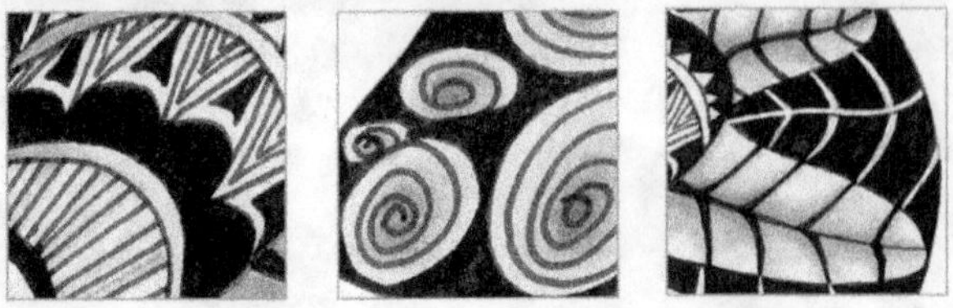

KOALA

The koala has a stout, tailless body; round, fluffy ears; and a large, spoon-shaped nose. It lives in eucalypt woodlands, and the leaves of these trees make up most of its diet. A koala can sleep up to 20 hours a day. Being a marsupial, a koala gives birth to underdeveloped young that crawl into their mother's pouch, where they stay for the first six to seven months of their lives. A young koala is known as a joey.

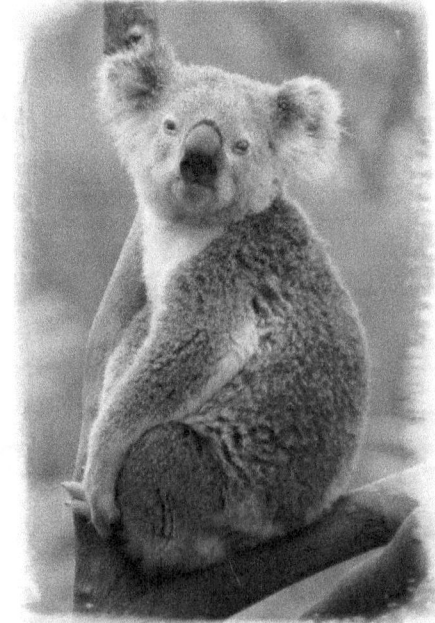

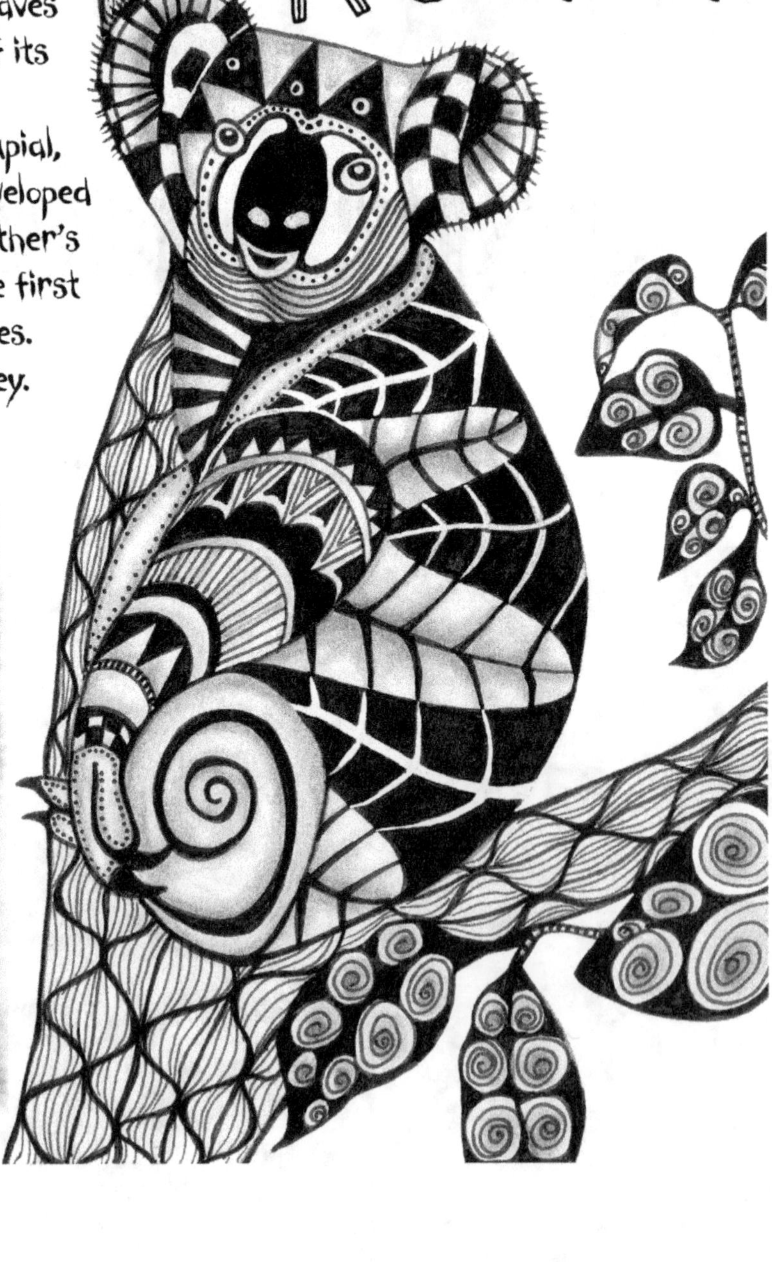

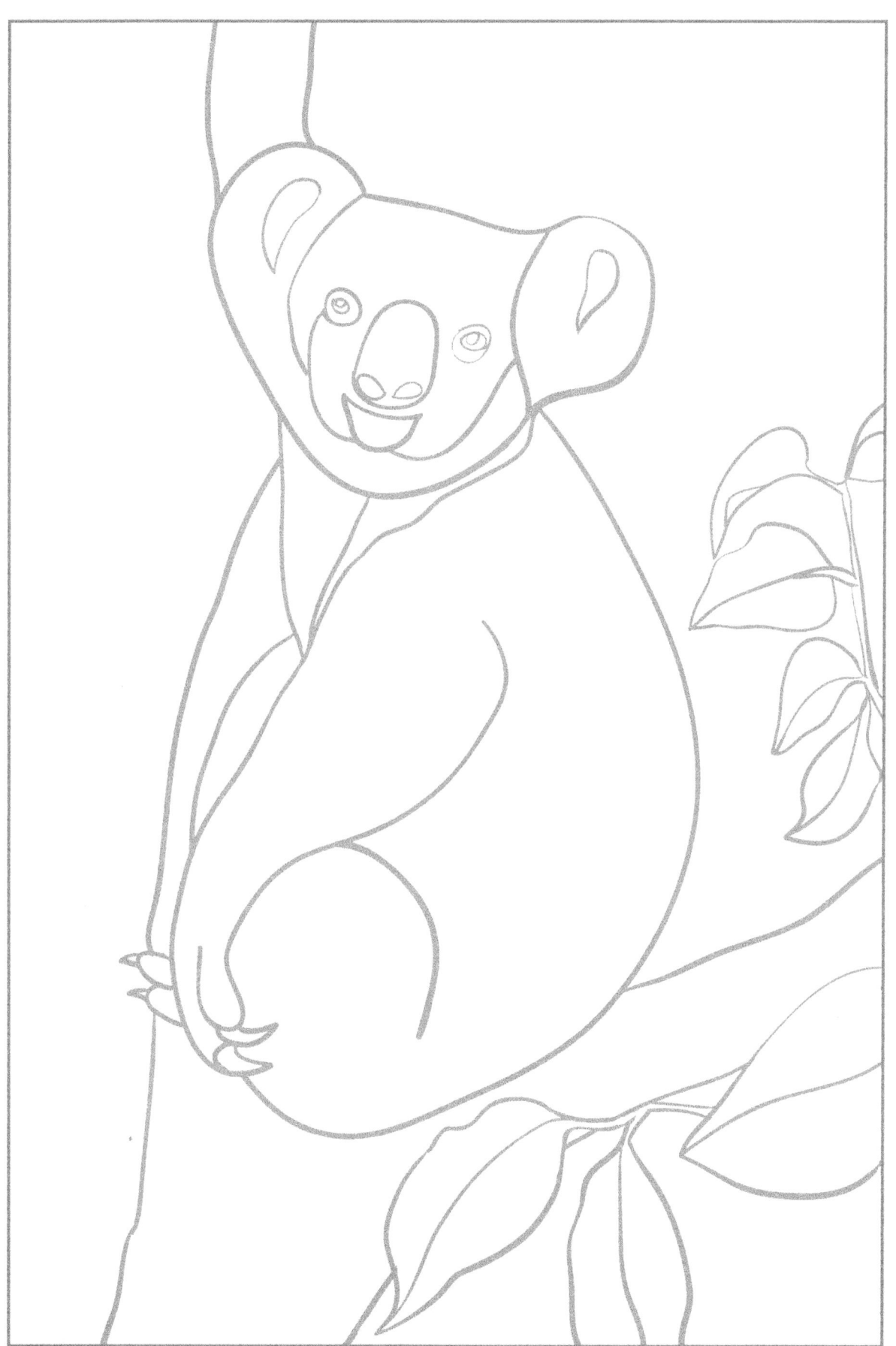

tangle a barn owl

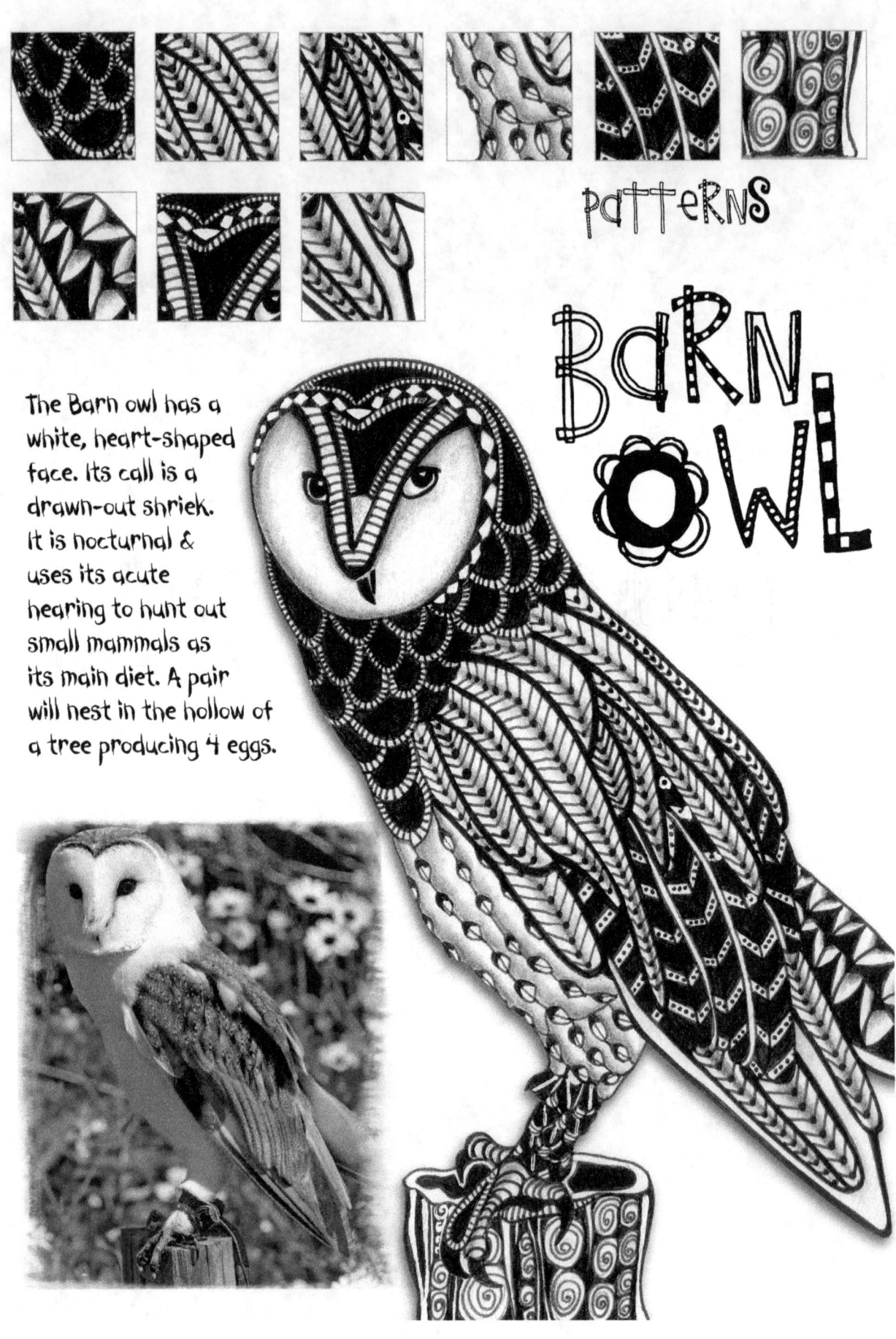

PATTERNS

BARN OWL

The Barn owl has a white, heart-shaped face. Its call is a drawn-out shriek. It is nocturnal & uses its acute hearing to hunt out small mammals as its main diet. A pair will nest in the hollow of a tree producing 4 eggs.

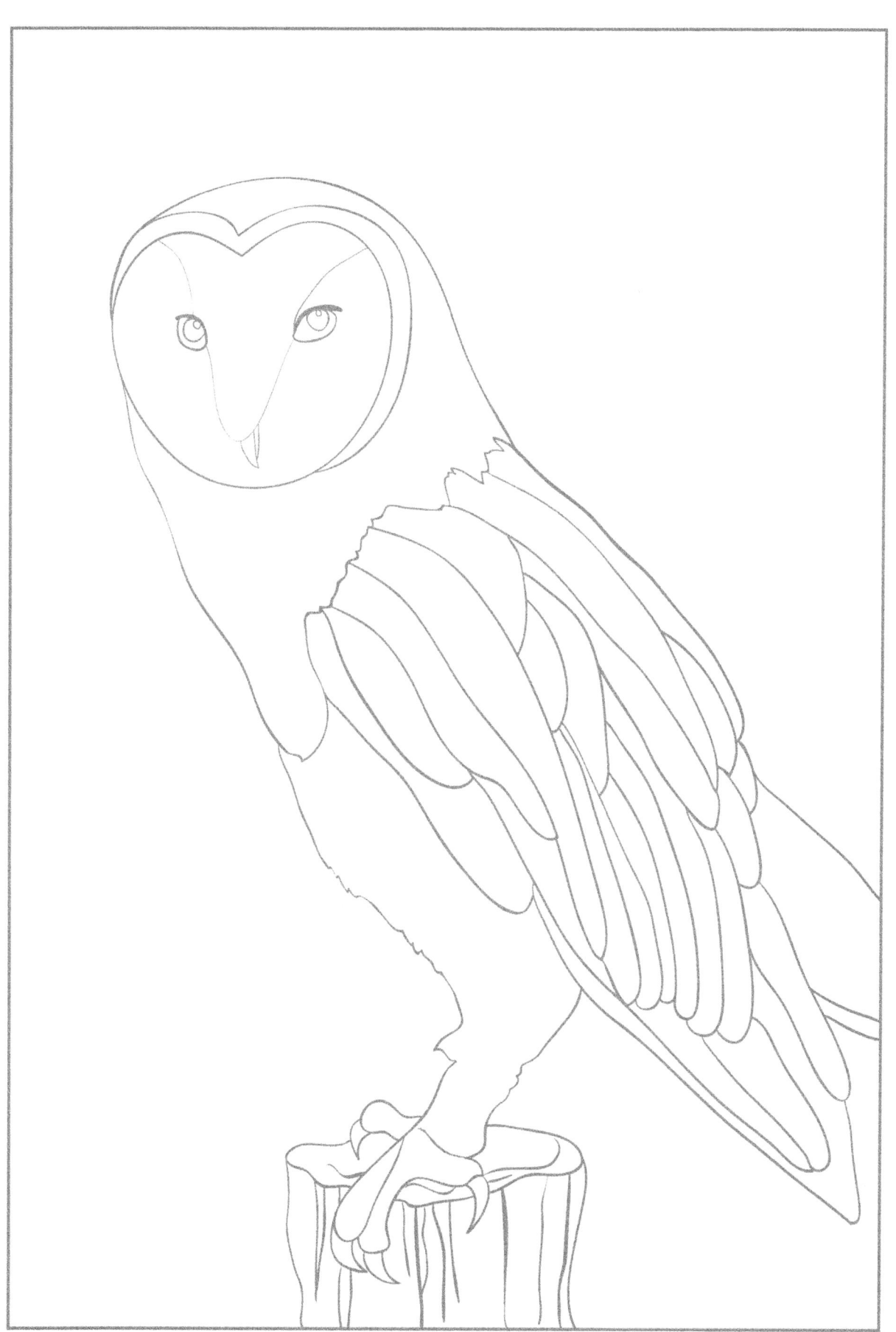

tangle a bat

PATTERNS

Bat

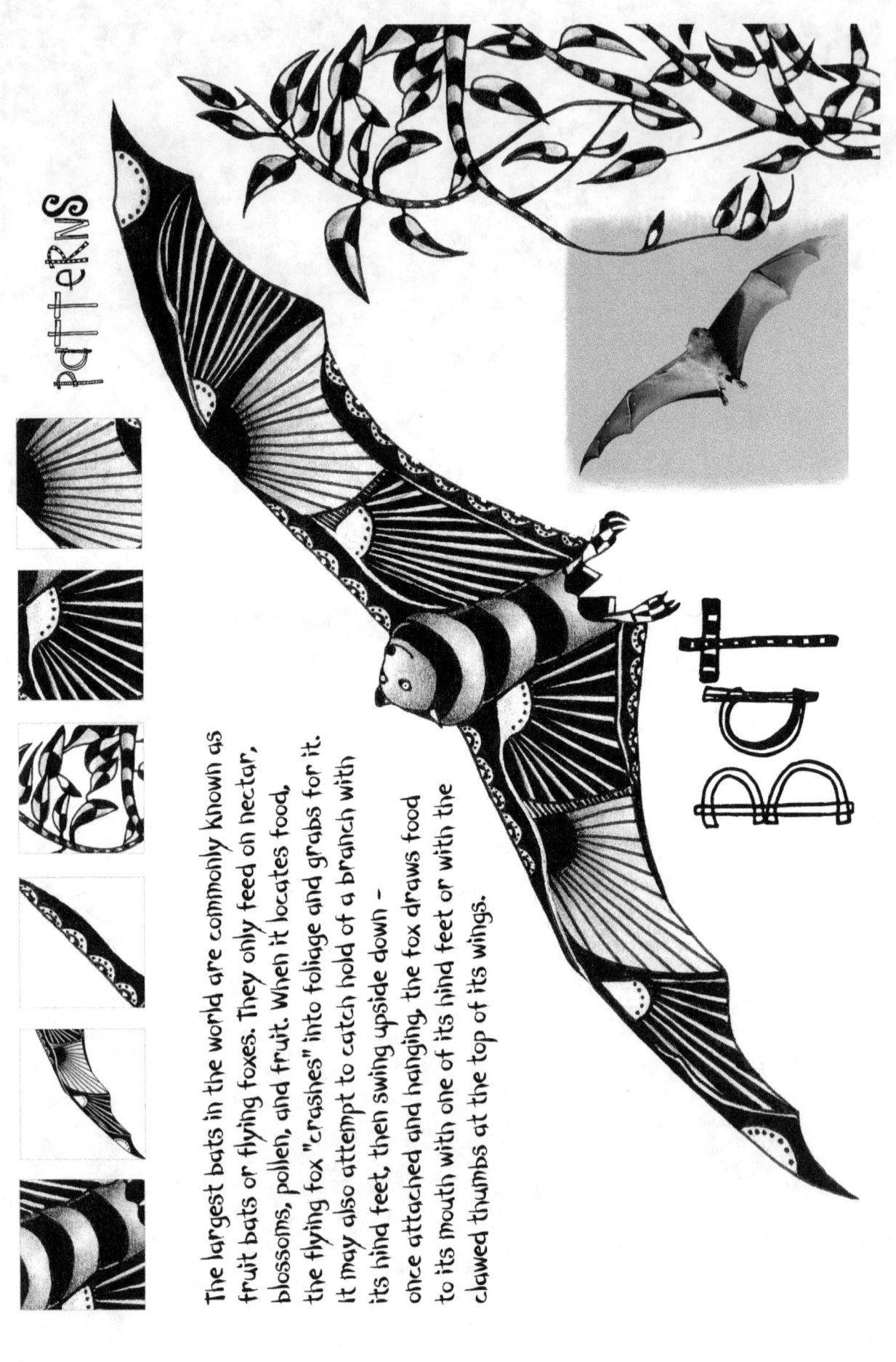

The largest bats in the world are commonly known as fruit bats or flying foxes. They only feed on nectar, blossoms, pollen, and fruit. When it locates food, the flying fox "crashes" into foliage and grabs for it. It may also attempt to catch hold of a branch with its hind feet, then swing upside down – once attached and hanging, the fox draws food to its mouth with one of its hind feet or with the clawed thumbs at the top of its wings.

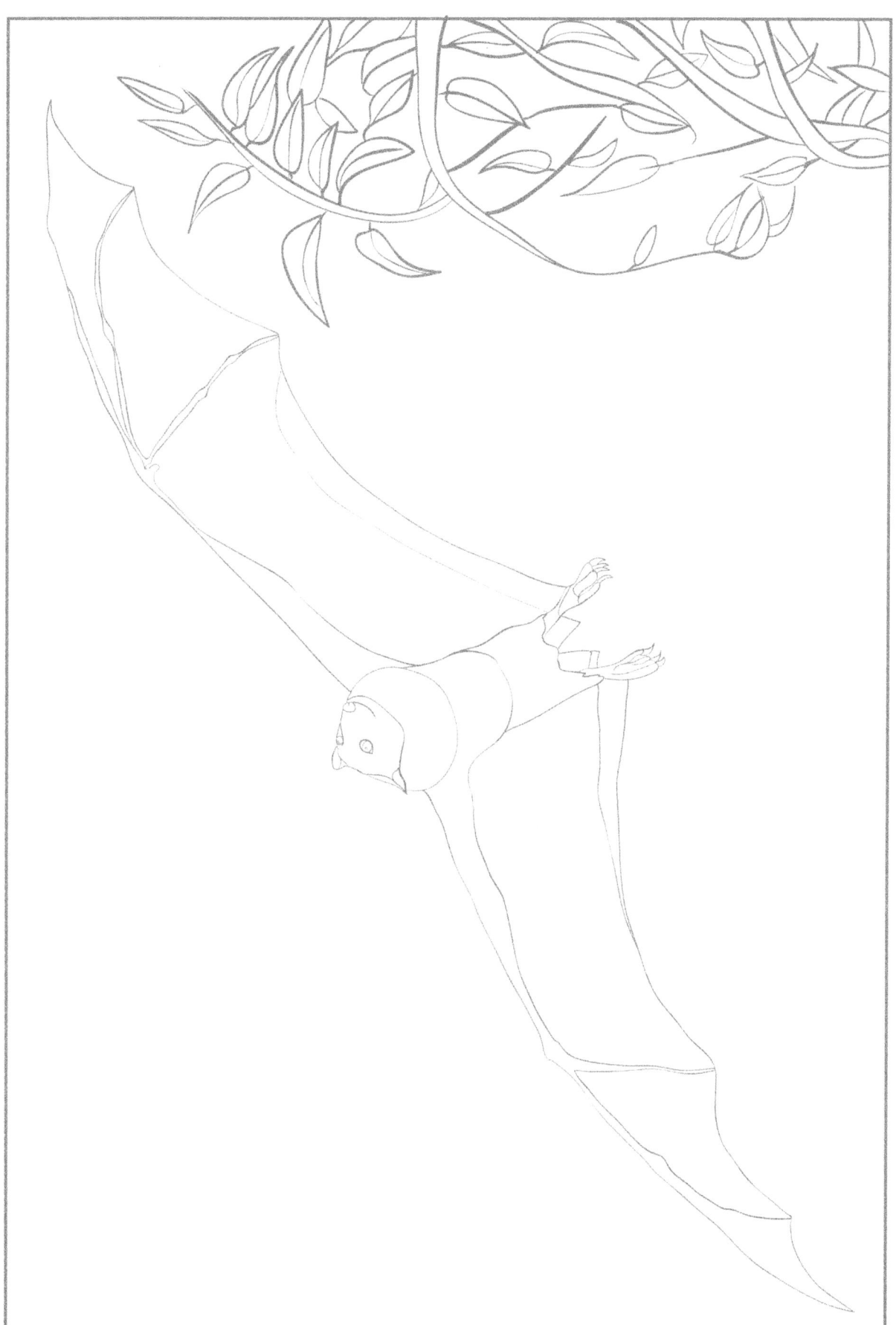

tangLe a caSSOwaRy

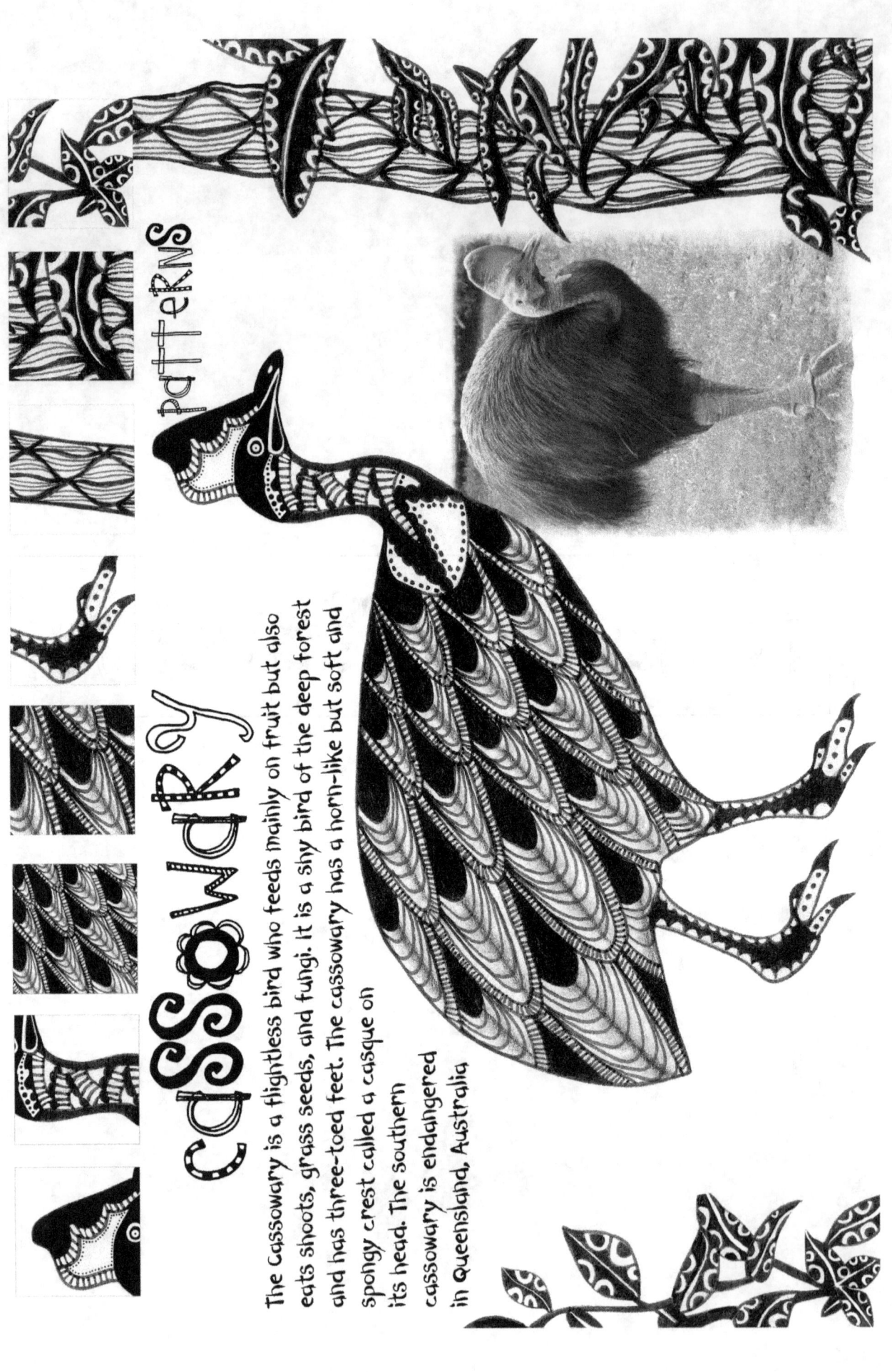

cassowary

patterns

The cassowary is a flightless bird who feeds mainly on fruit but also eats shoots, grass seeds, and fungi. It is a shy bird of the deep forest and has three-toed feet. The cassowary has a horn-like but soft and spongy crest called a casque on its head. The southern cassowary is endangered in Queensland, Australia.

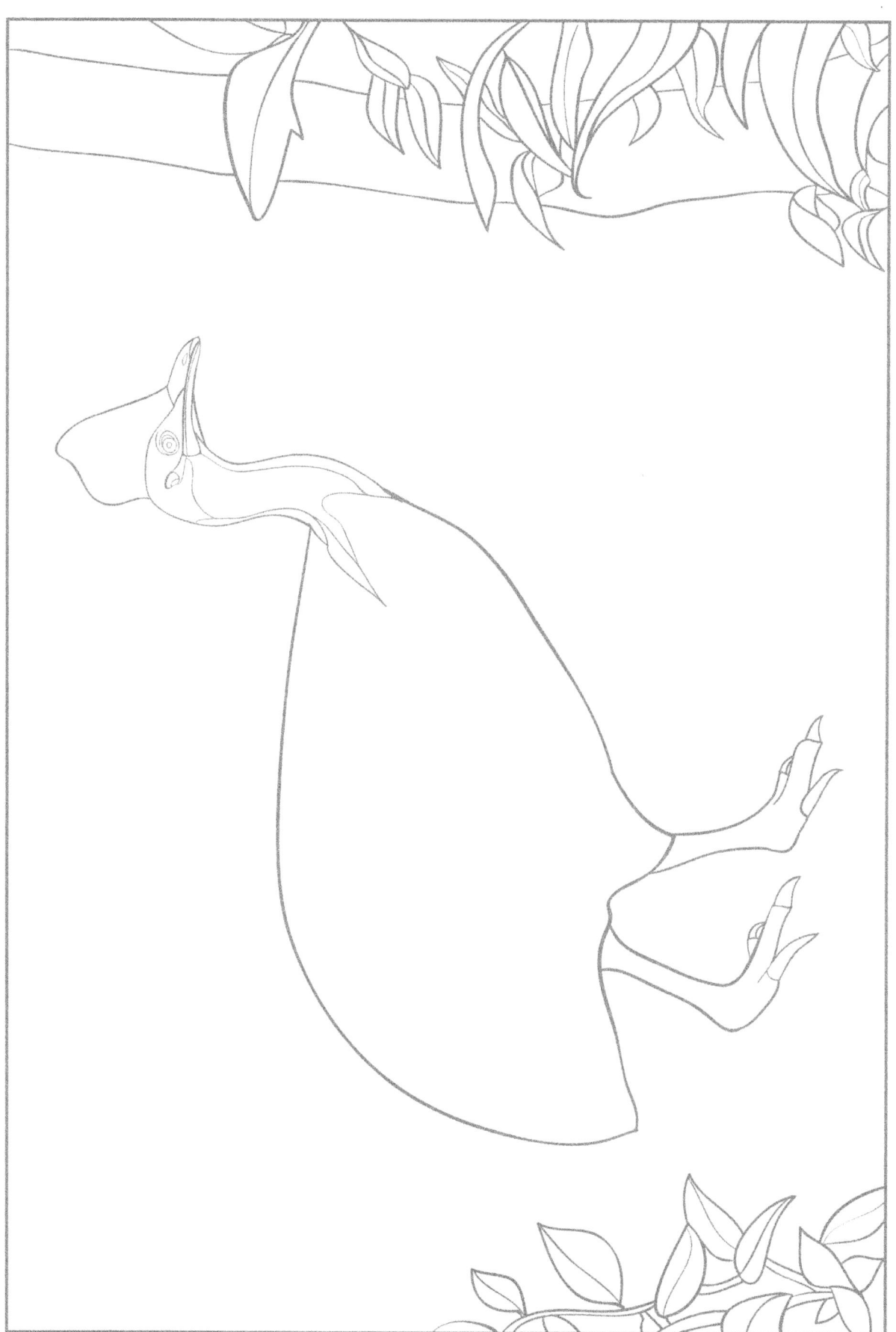

tANgLe a cRocodiLe

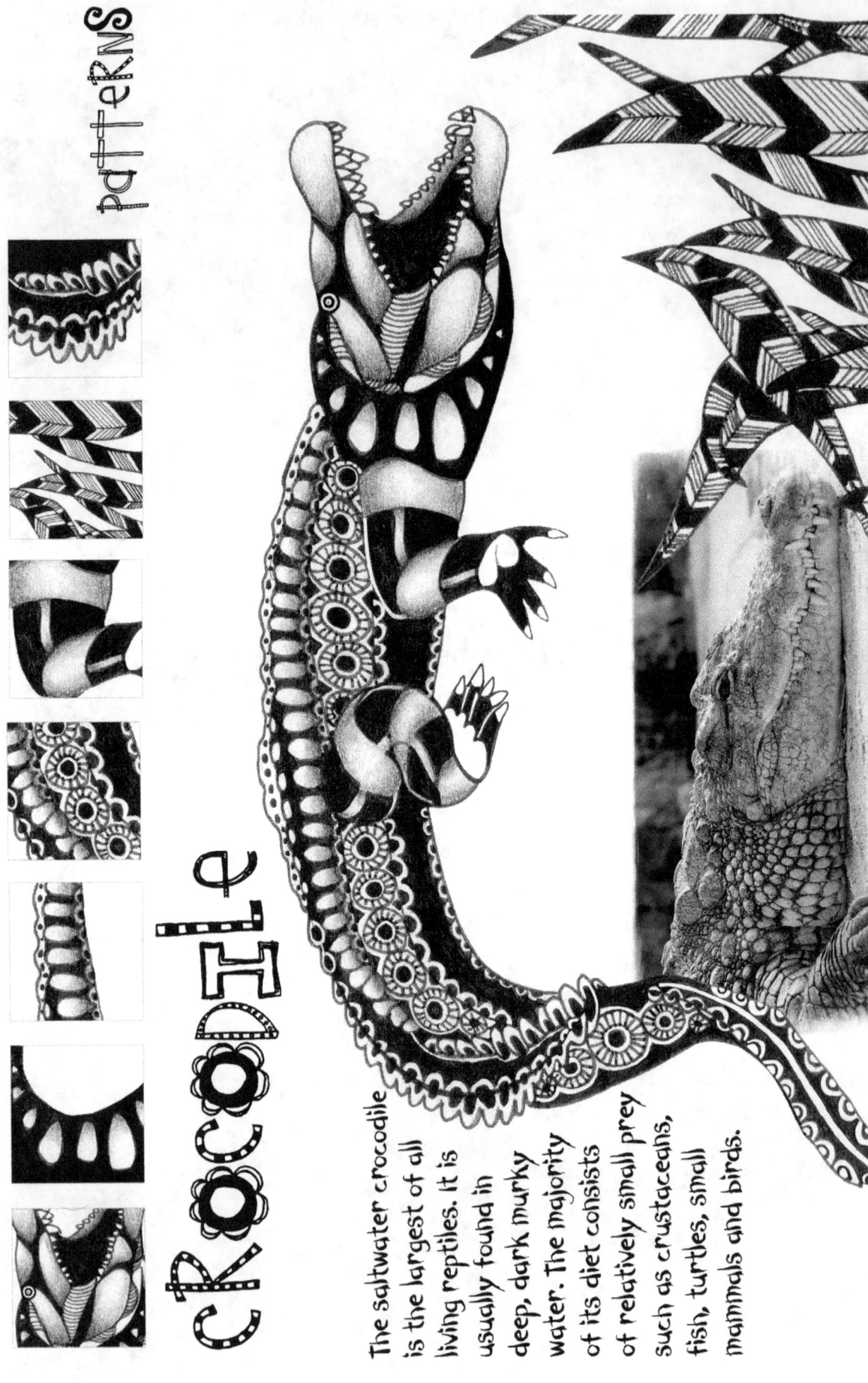

PATTERNS

CROCODILE

The saltwater crocodile is the largest of all living reptiles. It is usually found in deep, dark murky water. The majority of its diet consists of relatively small prey such as crustaceans, fish, turtles, small mammals and birds.

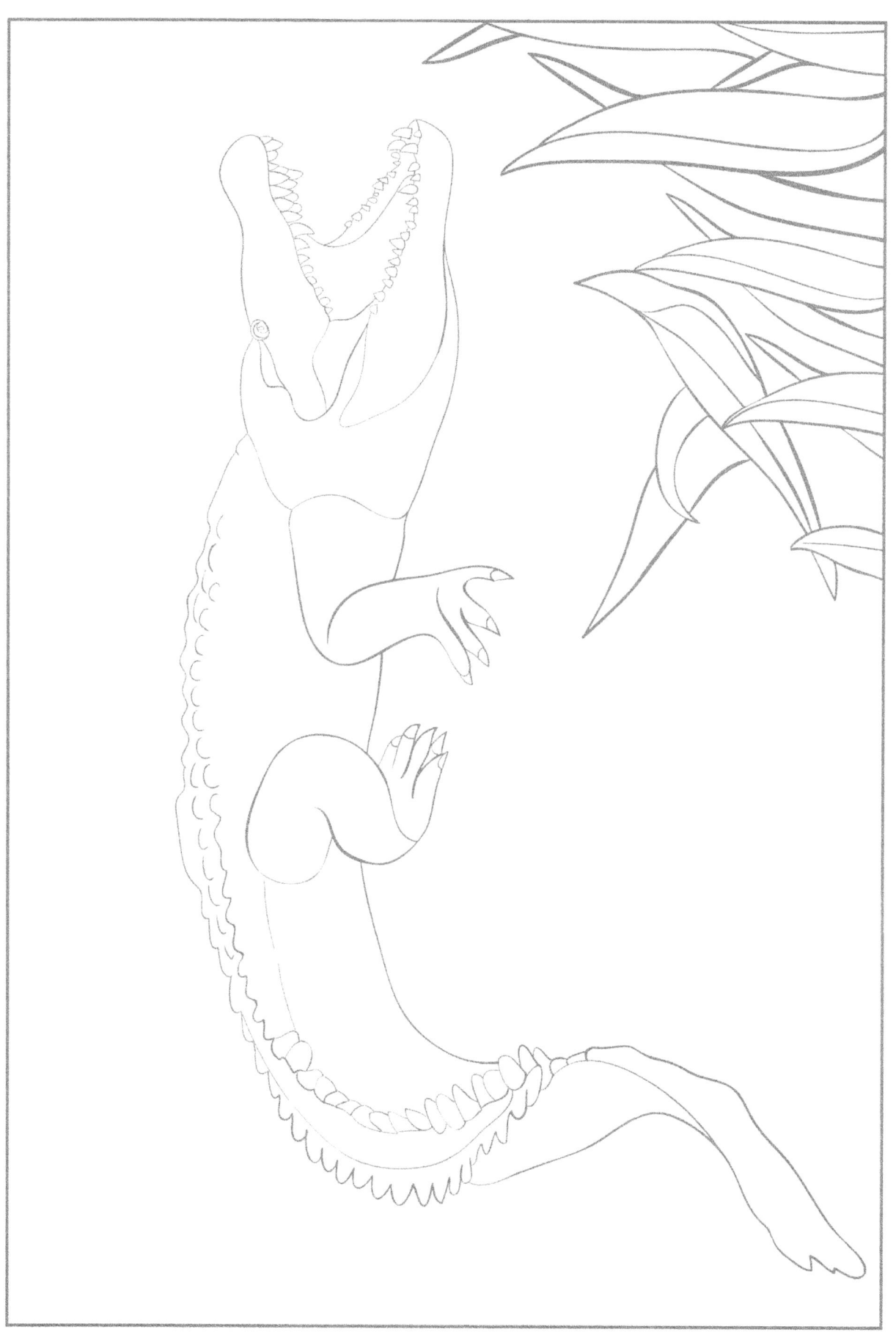

tangle a gecko

PATTERNS

geckos

Geckos are mostly nocturnal with soft bodies and tiny granular scales. They have well-developed limbs with five digits, large eyes with vertical pupils, no eyelids, and broad fleshy tongues. In the absence of eyelids, the tongue is used to lick the eye clean. Most are insect-eaters but sap and nectar are often included in their diets. Many species have expanded toe pads that provide grip and allow them to run on vertical or slippery surfaces.

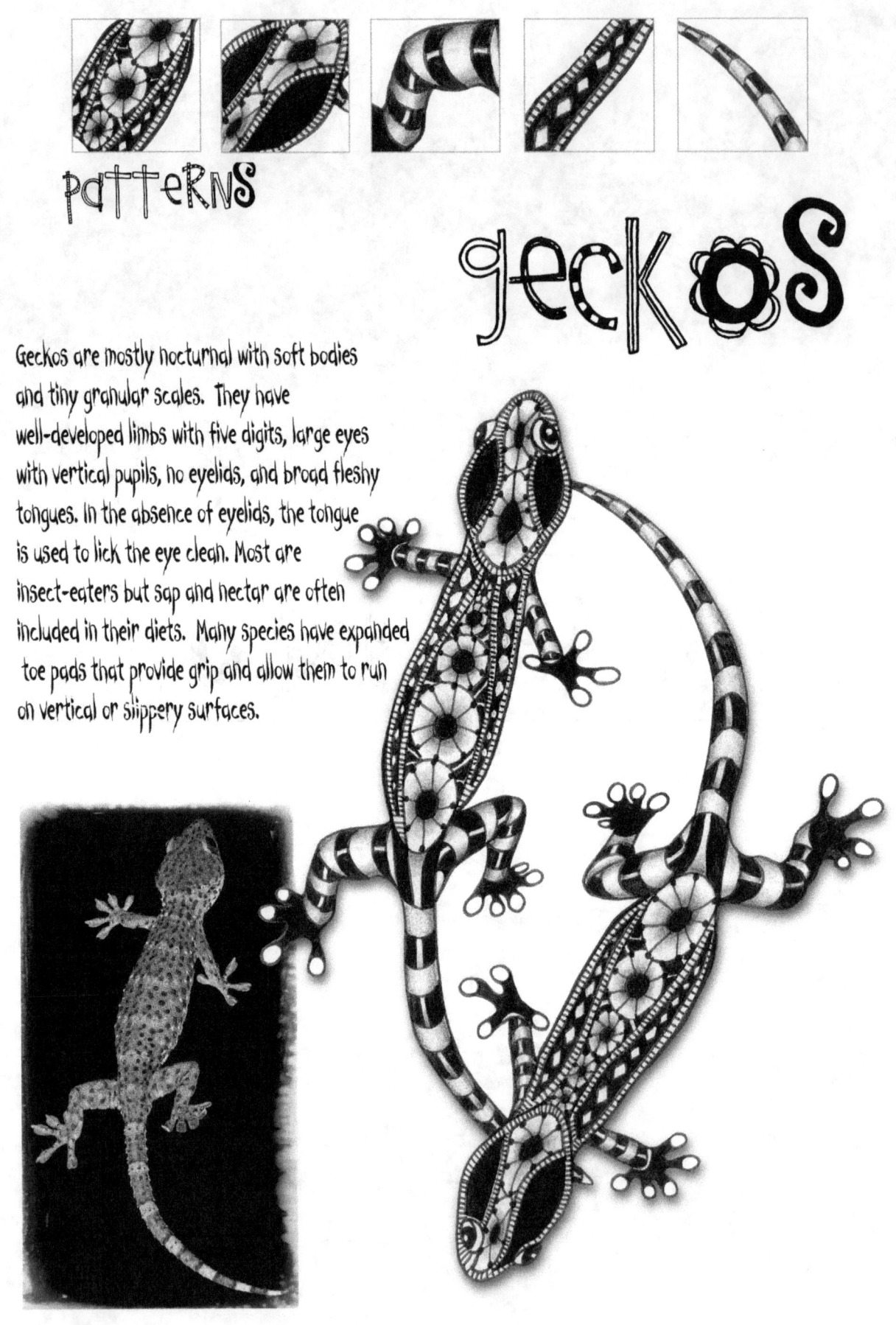

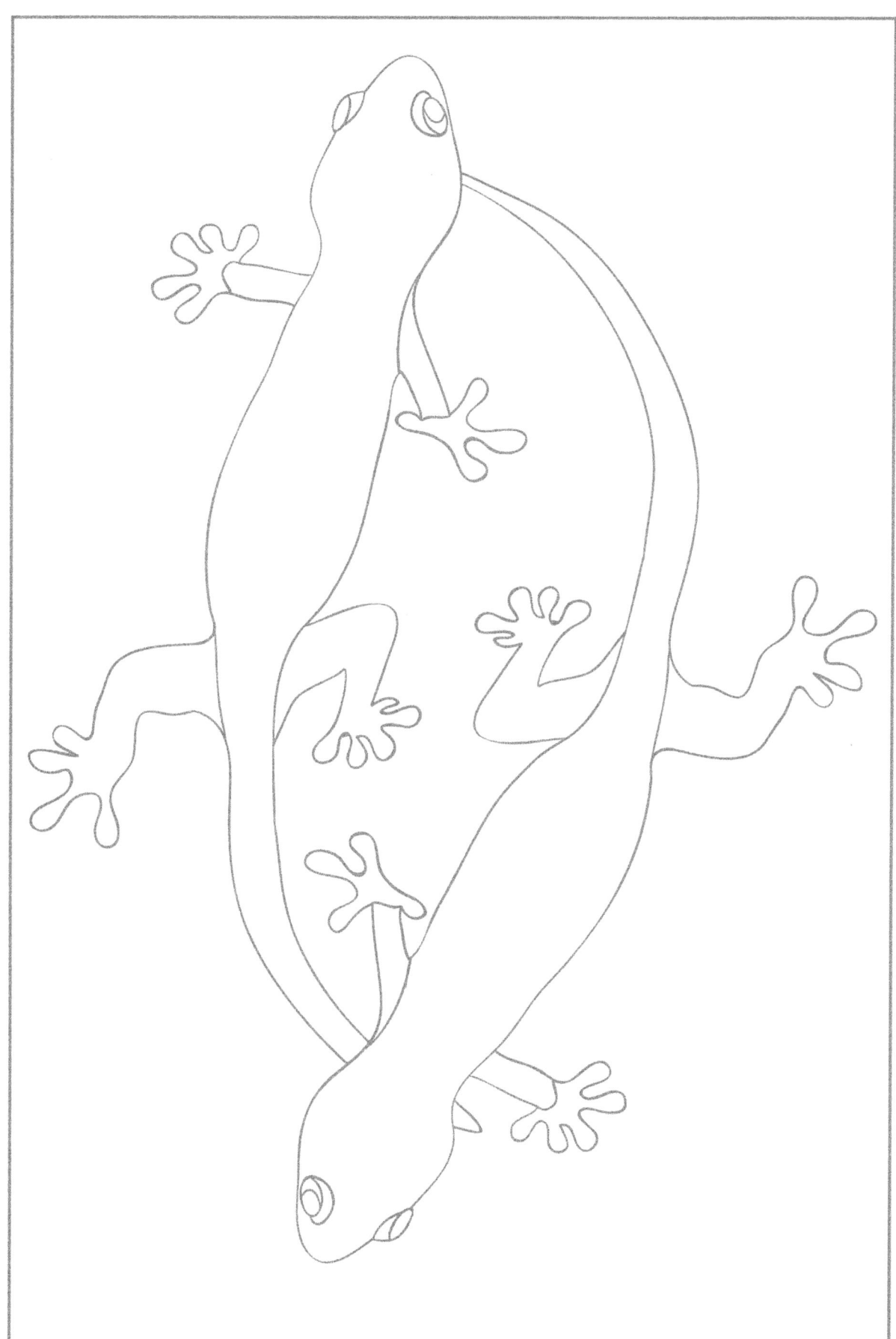

Tangle a Kangaroo

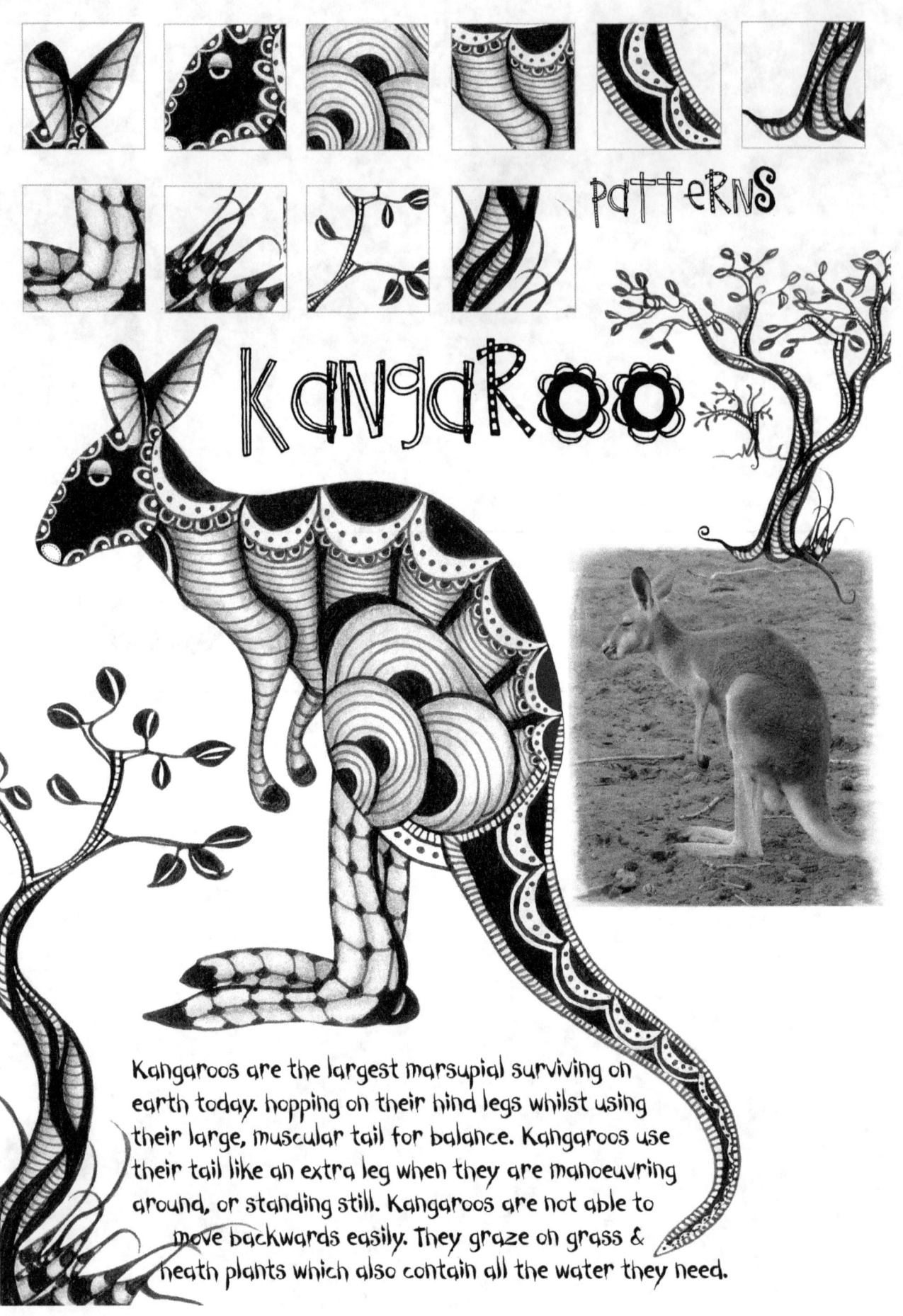

PATTERNS

KANgAROO

Kangaroos are the largest marsupial surviving on earth today. hopping on their hind legs whilst using their large, muscular tail for balance. Kangaroos use their tail like an extra leg when they are manoeuvring around, or standing still. Kangaroos are not able to move backwards easily. They graze on grass & heath plants which also contain all the water they need.

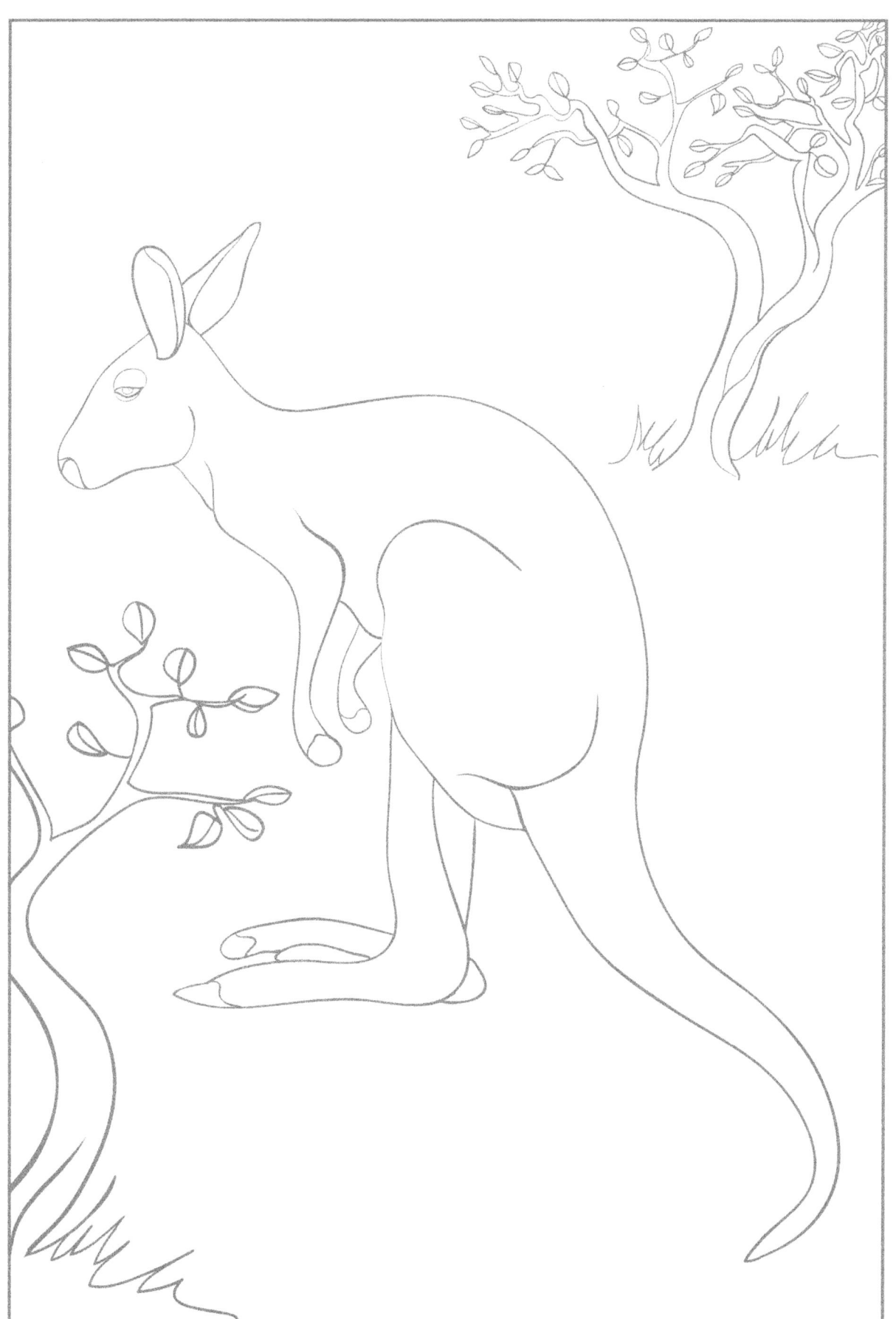

tangle a kookaburra

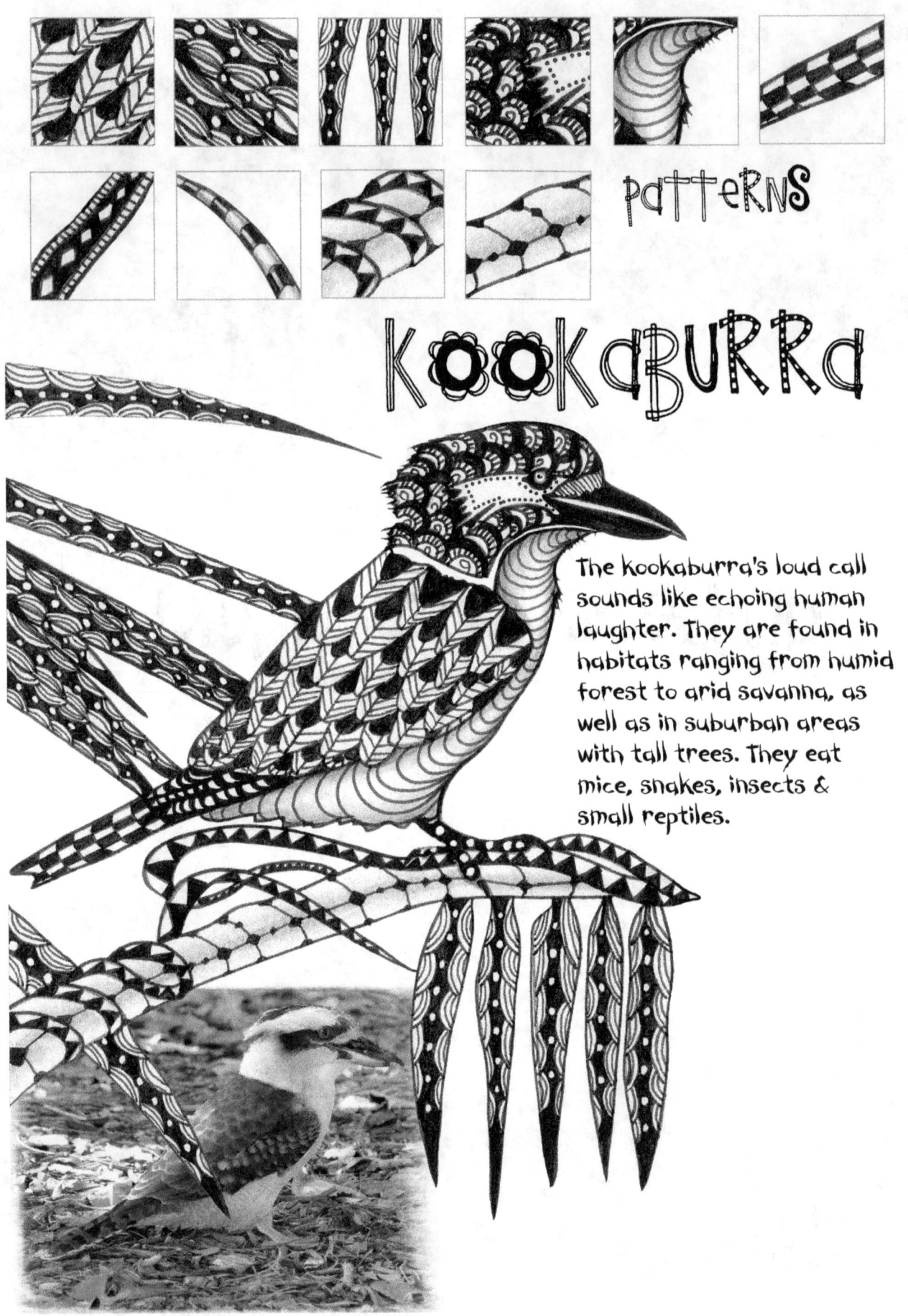

PATTERNS

KOOKABURRA

The kookaburra's loud call sounds like echoing human laughter. They are found in habitats ranging from humid forest to arid savanna, as well as in suburban areas with tall trees. They eat mice, snakes, insects & small reptiles.

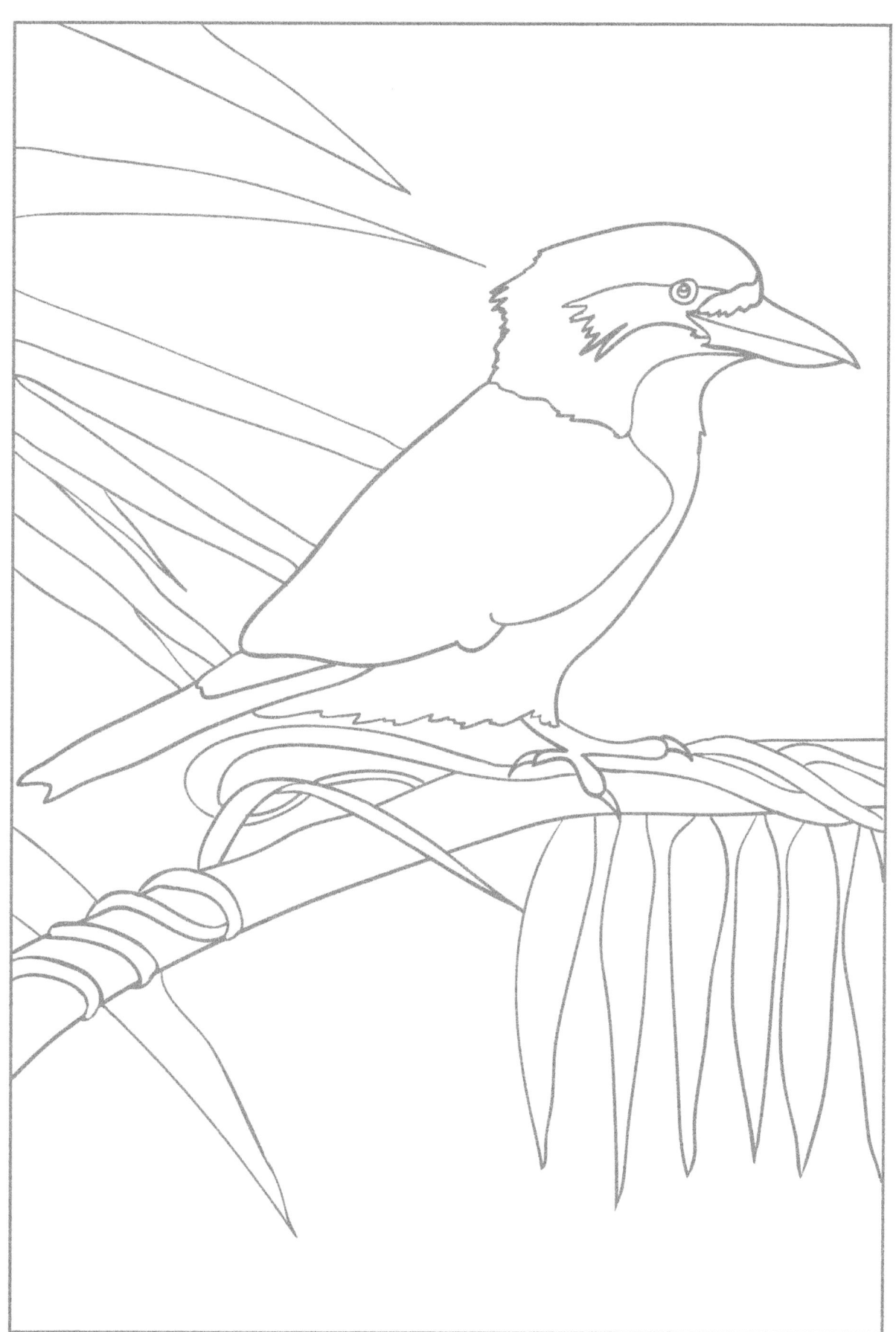

tangle a pelican

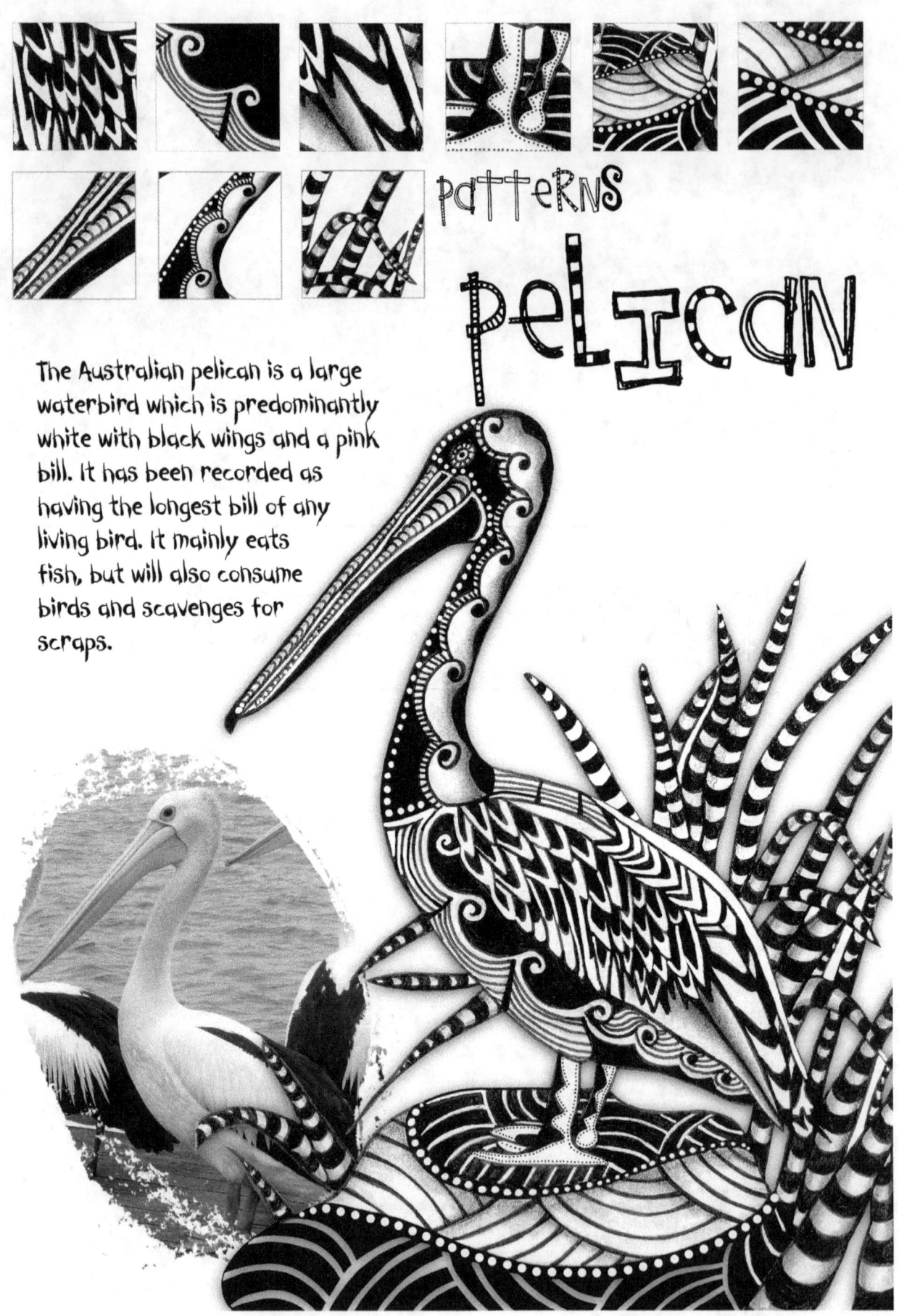

PATTERNS

PELICAN

The Australian pelican is a large waterbird which is predominantly white with black wings and a pink bill. It has been recorded as having the longest bill of any living bird. It mainly eats fish, but will also consume birds and scavenges for scraps.

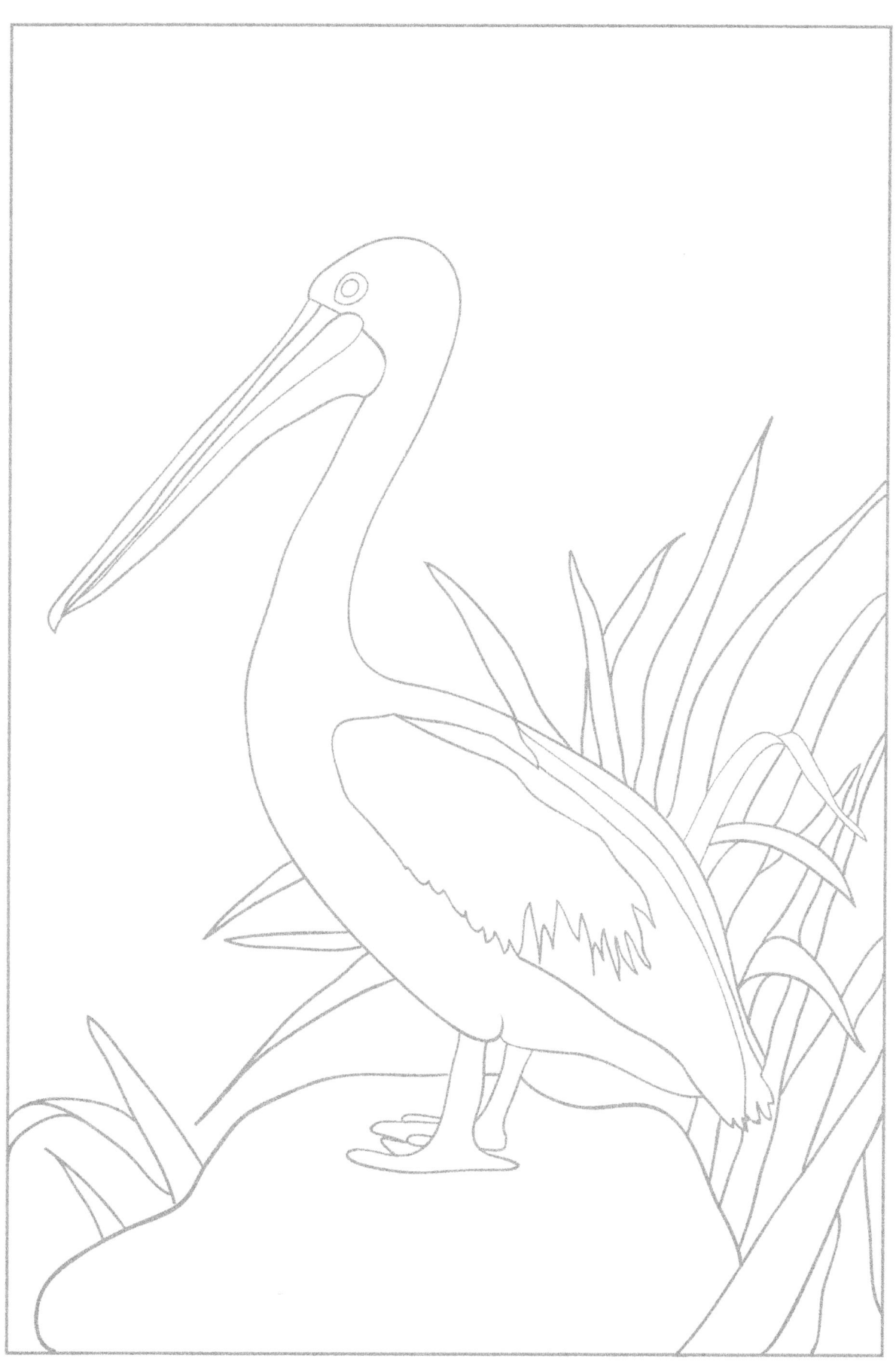

tangLe a poSSum

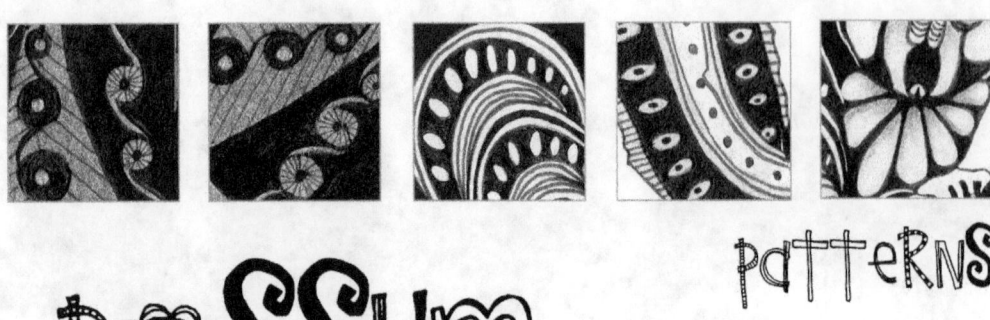

PATTERNS

POSSUM

The Common Brushtail Possum is the most widely distributed large possum species. They mainly inhabit areas of woodlands and open forests. In the wild, these Possums usually make a home in the hollow limbs of trees. They are also known for making their homes in roofs of houses and sheds in suburban areas. They eat leaves, grasses, herbs, flowers, fruits and insects.

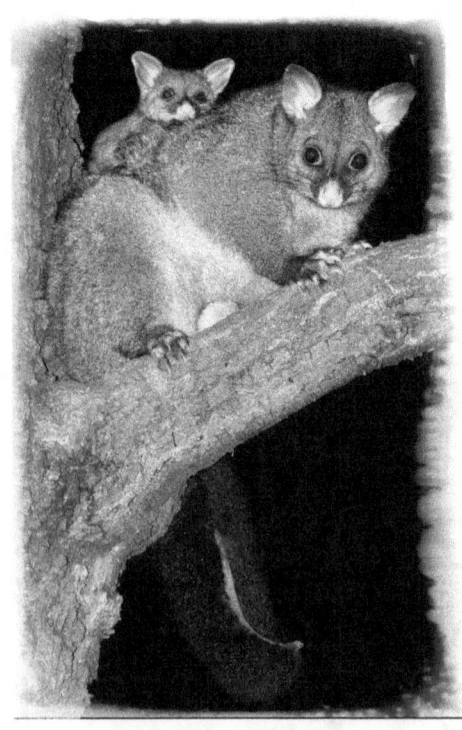

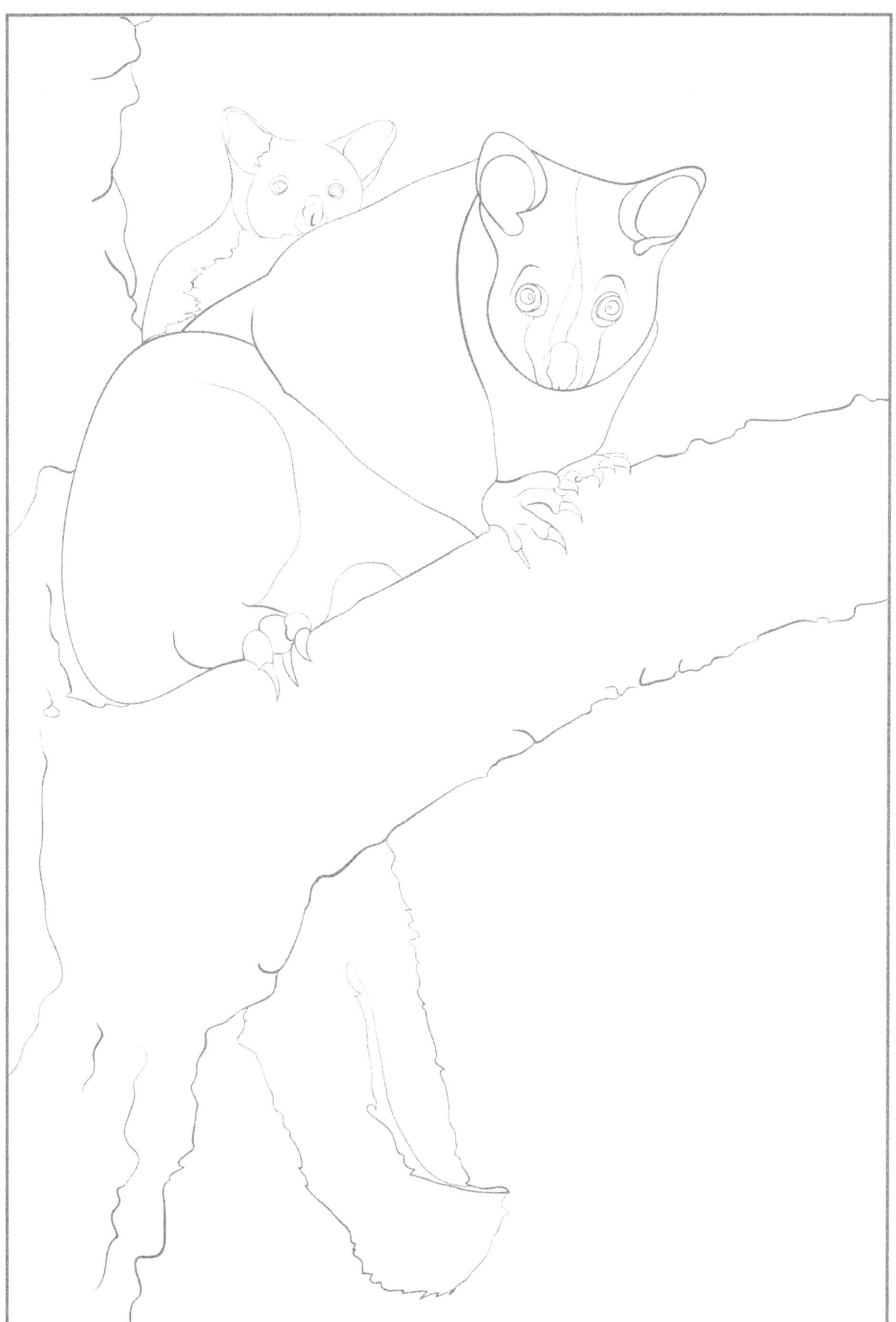

tangLe a TuRtLe

TURTLE

patterns

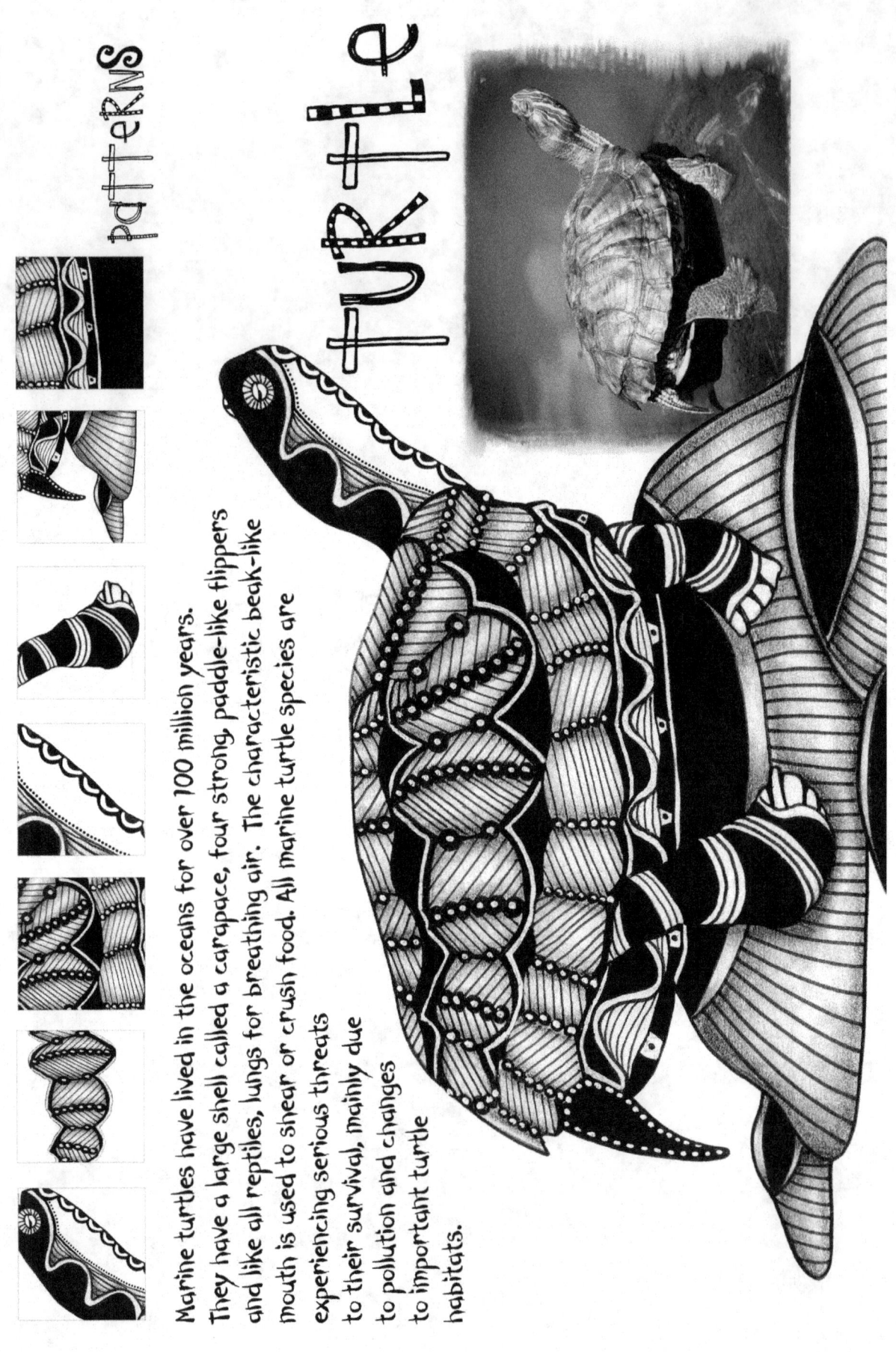

Marine turtles have lived in the oceans for over 100 million years. They have a large shell called a carapace, four strong, paddle-like flippers and like all reptiles, lungs for breathing air. The characteristic beak-like mouth is used to shear or crush food. All marine turtle species are experiencing serious threats to their survival, mainly due to pollution and changes to important turtle habitats.

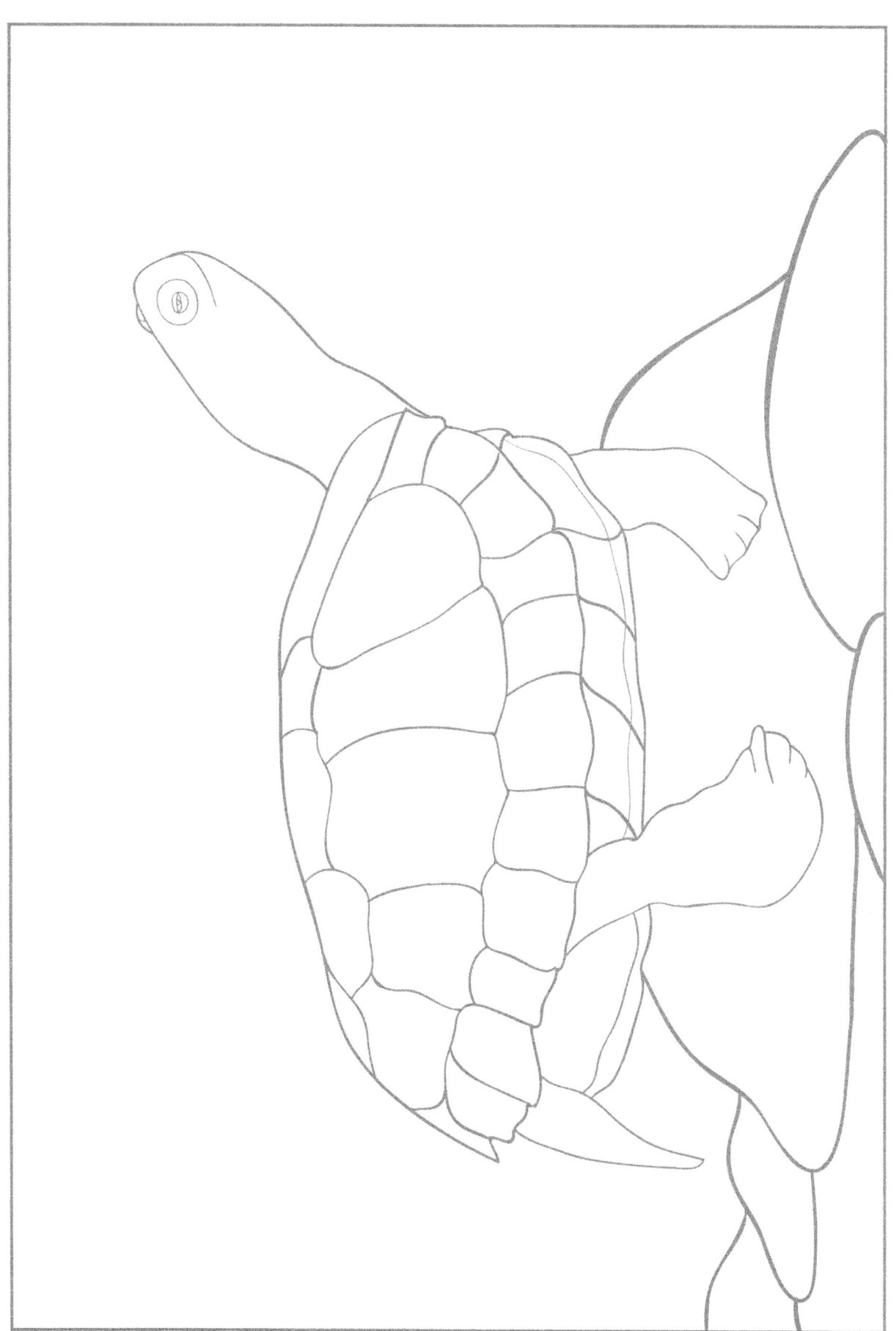

the end

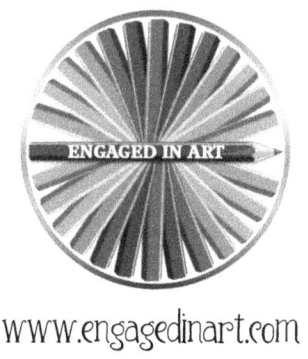